The Institute of Chartered Financial Analysts
Continuing Education Series

Valuation of Closely Held Companies and Inactively Traded Securities

December 5, 1989
Chicago, Illinois

Marko A. Budgyk
Frank C. Carr, Jr.
Gregory A. Gilbert, CFA
Chester A. Gougis

David W. Nicholas
Robert P. Oliver
Shannon P. Pratt, CFA
James G. Wolf, CFA

Edited by
E. Theodore Veit, CFA

Sponsored by
The Institute of Chartered
Financial Analysts

Additional copies of this publication may be ordered from:

Association for Investment Management and Research
P.O. Box 7947
Charlottesville, VA 22906
1-804-980-3647 (Phone)
1-804-977-0350 (Fax)

The Association for Investment Management and Research
comprises the Institute of Chartered Financial Analysts
and the Financial Analysts Federation.

Katrina F. Sherrerd, *Managing Editor*
Joni L. Tomal, *Associate Editor*
Diane B. Hamshar, *Typesetting/Layout*

ISBN 0-935015-19-1

Printed in the United States of America

Table of Contents

Foreword

Valuing a business is one of the fundamentals of investments. Most portfolio managers have concentrated on the valuation of firms whose shares are actively traded in public markets. The techniques involved in valuing closely held companies or inactively traded securities of publicly held companies are not as well known. In fact, the experts have not reached a consensus on the appropriate way to handle many of the issues that make the valuation of these interests so complicated.

Although the valuation of closely held companies and inactively traded securities fits into the same framework as the valuation of securities of publicly traded firms, there are substantial differences. Some of the characteristics peculiar to the valuation of closely held companies include a lack of relevant data; the need to reflect premia for controlling interests, discounts for minority interests, lack of marketability, and so forth; the need to conform to laws and regulations, such as IRS regulations, and state and federal laws; and the existence of legal precedents that dominate various aspects of valuations.

Traditionally, most of the demand for business appraisals came from buyers and sellers of small businesses and taxpayers attempting to establish the appropriate value for tax purposes. In many cases, regulatory agencies and courts were involved. More recently, portfolio managers have become interested in these valuations because of the growth in leveraged buyouts and venture capital investment opportunities.

To provide CFAs and other interested parties with a general overview of the methods employed in the valuation of closely held companies and inactively traded securities, the Institute of Chartered Financial Analysts sponsored a one-day seminar on this topic in Chicago on December 5, 1989. The proceedings of that seminar provide a valuable source of information on the key issues to be considered in the valuation of closely held companies and inactively traded securities, and the techniques employed by professionals who are actively engaged in this specialized field.

The seminar brought together an impressive group of experts. The Association for Investment Management and Research (AIMR) wishes to extend its sincere appreciation to the seminar speakers. Special thanks are extended to Shannon P. Pratt, CFA, Willamette Management Associates, Inc., who acted as both moderator and speaker. Other speakers included Marko A. Budgyk, Houlihan, Lokey, Howard & Zukin, Inc.; Frank C. Carr, Jr., Ernst & Young; Gregory A. Gilbert, CFA, Corporate Valuations, Inc.; Chester A. Gougis, Duff & Phelps Financial Consulting Co.; David W. Nicholas, Ernst & Young; Robert P. Oliver, Management Planning, Inc.; and James G. Wolf, CFA, Ernst & Young. AIMR wishes to extend its appreciation to all of the speakers who participated in this seminar and assisted in the publication of these proceedings.

Several other individuals also contributed to the production of these proceedings. The program was organized by Susan D. Martin, CFA, Vice President, AIMR, with valuable input from Darwin M. Bayston, CFA, Executive Vice President, AIMR, Shannon P. Pratt, CFA, and James G. Wolf, CFA. We would also like to thank E. Theodore Veit, CFA, Rollins College, for his contributions to the development of the program and the publication of these proceedings.

Katrina F. Sherrerd
Vice President
Research and Publications
Association for Investment
Management and Research

Biographies of Speakers

Marko A. Budgyk is President and Chief Investment Officer of Houlihan, Lokey, Howard & Zukin Investment Management, Inc. and Vice President of Houlihan, Lokey, Howard & Zukin, Inc. Prior to joining the firm, he held analyst positions with Xerox and Tosco corporations. He is a general securities representative with the National Association of Securities Dealers, Inc. Mr. Budgyk holds a B.A. from Pomona College and an M.B.A. from the University of Chicago.

Frank C. Carr, Jr. is Senior Manager of Ernst & Young. He was formerly manager of the financial valuation group of American Appraisal Associates, a firm with which he has been associated for 11 years. Mr. Carr is a senior member of the American Society of Appraisers (ASA) and a member of the Valuation Advisory Committee of the Employee Stock Ownership Plan Association. He is a faculty member of the ASA Valuation Institute and a guest lecturer at Marquette University. Mr. Carr holds a B.A. from Stanford University.

Gregory A. Gilbert, CFA is President of Corporate Valuations, Inc. He is a senior member of the American Society of Appraisers (ASA) and serves as northwest regional governor and a member of the Business Valuation Committee. Prior to joining Corporate Valuations in 1983, Mr. Gilbert was vice president and associate director of research with Willamette Management Associates, Inc. He holds a B.A. from Yale University and an M.S. from Massachusetts Institute of Technology.

Chester A. Gougis is an Executive Vice President of Duff & Phelps Inc. and Managing Director of its wholly owned subsidiary, Duff & Phelps Financial Consulting Co. Mr. Gougis has published several articles on financial and valuation topics in *The National Law Journal* and has served as an expert witness in a number of major court cases. He is a member of the Valuation Study Group, the Employee Stock Ownership Plan Association, the Economics Club of Chicago, and the Business Valuation Association. Mr. Gougis holds a B.A. from Harvard University and an M.B.A. from the University of Chicago.

David W. Nicholas is a Director with Ernst & Young. Previously, he was a vice president with American Appraisal Associates' National Practice Office. Mr. Nicholas specializes in the valuation of business enterprises, including underlying tangible and intangible assets and corporate securities. He has prepared documentation and testimony for regulatory and legislative hearings and has qualified as an expert witness and offered testimony in several states. A senior member of the American Society of Appraisers and a member of its Business Valuation Committee, he is a regular speaker for a number of organizations. Mr. Nicholas holds an M.B.A. from the University of Chicago.

Robert P. Oliver is Vice President and a member of the Board of Directors of Management Planning, Inc. He is a senior member of the American Society of Appraisers and a member of the ASA Business Valuation Committee. An adjunct professor of finance at Trenton State College, Mr. Oliver holds a B.A. from Rutgers College and an M.B.A. from New York University.

Shannon P. Pratt, CFA is President of Willamette Management Associates, Inc. He is a Fellow and senior member of the American Society of Appraisers. Dr. Pratt is the author of two books, *Valuing a Business: The Analysis and Appraisal of Closely Held Companies* and *Valuing Small Businesses and Professional Practices*, as well as numerous articles. He holds a Ph.D. from Indiana University.

James G. Wolf, CFA is a Senior Manager in the Valuation Services Group of Ernst & Young. He is a member of the Employee Stock Ownership Valuation Advisory Committee of the Employee Stock Ownership Plan Association, a member of the Financial Analysts Federation, and a Commercial Arbitration Panel member of the American Arbitration Association. Mr. Wolf has provided deposition and expert witness testimony in Texas and has participated in the preparation of expert witness testimony for valuation cases litigated in Oklahoma and Texas. He holds a B.B.A. from the University of Notre Dame and an M.B.A. from the University of Texas-Austin.

Overview of the Seminar

E. Theodore Veit, CFA

Valuation of closely held companies and inactively traded securities is a large and growing business, but it remains virtually unknown to the public. There are several reasons why most of the public and much of the investment community knows little about this important activity. One reason relates to the very nature of the business: Because the firms and securities being valued are closely held, the public is generally unaware that such valuations are taking place. Additionally, because closely held firms tend to be smaller than publicly traded firms, fewer investors are affected by the results of such valuations. Finally, the reasons for conducting valuations of closely held firms frequently involve private transactions such as property settlements, damage cases, tax liability determinations, and acquisitions and mergers of private companies—all of which receive little publicity.

Valuation of closely held companies and inactively traded securities is being performed by professionals with a wide range of backgrounds. The ideal practitioner in this business would have extensive experience in securities analysis, an activity that can provide a sound understanding of the process of valuing *publicly* traded securities, because the framework used by securities analysts is basically the same as the framework used in the valuation of closely held companies and inactively traded securities. The ideal practitioner would also have a background in accounting, because much of the valuation process involves the interpretation and adjustment of financial statements and forecasts of income and cash flows. The need for specialized backgrounds does not stop there, however. The ideal practitioner would also have a background in real estate appraisal (businesses being valued frequently have substantial real estate holdings); a background in the appraisal of fixed assets (the value of a firm's assets is frequently viewed as a major source of firm value); and a specialized background in adjusting business values for such things as lack of marketability and premium for control interest.

On December 5, 1989, a seminar was held in Chicago to address important issues and provide a forum for an exchange of information and ideas related to the valuation of closely held companies and inactively traded securities. That conference, or-

ganized and sponsored by the Institute of Chartered Financial Analysts (ICFA), led to the publication of these proceedings. The seminar and the proceedings were designed to appeal to CFAs, CFA candidates, valuation professionals with other backgrounds, attorneys, and other interested parties. To accomplish this, valuation professionals with varied backgrounds and from a variety of firms that perform business valuations were gathered to share their expertise with those in attendance. All of these professionals are industry leaders and known experts in their field.

It is hoped that the influence of this seminar on those who participate in the valuation of closely held companies and inactively traded securities will extend well beyond the individuals who were able to attend. Because the industry is growing, and because the techniques are similar to those applied to the valuation of publicly traded companies, it is expected that an increasing number of CFAs will find themselves actively engaged in this activity. These proceedings provide valuable insight into these activities.

The Legal Environment and Its Impact on Valuation

A large proportion of business valuations are conducted to address legal matters such as estate and gift taxes, state dissenters' rights, income taxes, divorce, and family and partnership disagreements. Legal proceedings in such matters have resulted in a substantial amount of case law with which business appraisers must be familiar. Additionally, although the Internal Revenue Service issued Revenue Ruling 59-60 some 30 years ago, the ruling continues to provide useful guidelines for conducting business valuations for estate- and gift-tax purposes. In fact, it was later expanded to cover the valuation of stock of closely held companies for all tax purposes.

In this presentation, Robert Oliver provides an overview of both relevant case law and Revenue Ruling 59-60. Every business appraiser must be familiar with this legal environment, not only because of the possibility of scrutiny by the courts, but also because the courts and the IRS have done an excellent job of identifying practical tools for conducting business valuations.

Market Approach to Valuation

Valuing a business using the market approach is one of the most popular and theoretically sound approaches to the valuation of closely held companies. In this presentation, James Wolf describes the steps an analyst must take to value the firm using this method. These steps include analyzing the economy, the subject firm's industry, and the subject firm itself; selecting and analyzing comparable publicly traded firms; adjusting the financial statements of both the subject firm and the comparable firms; analyzing the multiples of all firms involved; and selecting an appropriate multiple for the subject firm. The final step involves combining this information to determine the value of the firm. Wolf presents a brief case analysis to demonstrate some of the techniques he presents.

Discounted-Cash-Flow Approach to Valuation

Determining the value of a firm by finding the present value of all of its expected future cash flows is a popular valuation technique. Although theoretically sound, this technique is fraught with potential dangers if not employed correctly. In this section, Gregory Gilbert describes how to employ this valuation method. He begins by describing two basic discounted-cash-flow models and how they are employed. He then discusses how to estimate important input variables, including the difficult task of forecasting future cash flows. This can be particularly difficult because it involves evaluating historical cash flows, normalizing them, and then projecting them into the future. Gilbert concludes with a discussion of how to determine an appropriate discount rate and how to forecast a terminal value, if necessary.

Adjusted-Book-Value Approach to Valuation

The third and final valuation technique presented at the seminar involves the determination of the book value of a firm, where the accounting book value is adjusted to reflect the going-concern, fair market value of all the firm's assets and liabilities. David Nicholas guides the reader through the balance sheet one asset and liability at a time, describing the key determinants of book-value adjustment for each. He also describes how to determine the value of intangible assets, and when it is appropriate to do so. Nicholas then discusses how to pull together the adjusted assets and liabilities to determine the value of the firm. Because this valuation method is not appropriate in all situations, some general guidelines are offered to help determine when this technique should be used.

Discounts and Premia

Once the value of a firm has been determined using one of the techniques described above (or some other technique), an analyst should consider adjusting the value of the firm for lack of marketability or for the level of control commensurate with the interest being valued. In this session, Shannon Pratt reviews precedent-setting court cases and the results of empirical studies that specify the key variables influencing the size of marketability discounts. This discussion includes tables indicating the size of marketability discounts historically on a percentage basis.

Next, Pratt presents similar historical information about adjustments made to the value of businesses based on the level of control implied by the interest being valued. This area is particularly difficult for an analyst because many different factors can affect the level of control in a given situation. Pratt concludes with a brief discussion of additional reasons why discounts (key-person discounts, portfolio discounts, and so forth) may be taken.

Fairness and Solvency Opinions

The purpose of a fairness opinion generally is to provide a fiduciary with an independent opinion as to the value of the assets the fiduciary intends to sell. This opinion is obtained to establish the fairness of the selling price. For example, the board of directors of a company may elect to commission a fairness opinion to establish the value of the company before authorizing its sale. This may help verify for the shareholders that the sale price is fair.

Solvency opinions differ from fairness opinions in that they are typically obtained to protect the secured lenders, the corporate directors, and the shareholders of the selling firm from potential claims of fraudulent conveyance. Fraudulent conveyance could be involved if a firm has been sold at such a low price that unsecured creditors have an excessive exposure to the risk of firm insolvency.

In this section, Chester Gougis describes the intricacies and pitfalls of fairness and solvency opinions. Included in this discussion are a review of the legal and regulatory requirements of fairness opinions and a discussion of the impact of minority versus majority interests on the valuation process as it concerns fairness and solvency opinions.

Preferred Stocks, Bonds, and Specialized Securities

In this session, Marko Budgyk presents methods of valuing inactively traded securities other than common stock. The discussion identifies the key determinants of value, addresses how to determine an appropriate discount rate, and explores the various models used in the valuation of these securities.

The Appraisal Report: Current Standards, Proper Format, and Common Errors

Frank Carr addresses the necessary administrative details involved in writing a complete appraisal report. Although such matters may appear to be routine, experience suggests that many business valuations are presented so ineffectively that they become useless. Carr outlines and discusses the minimum required standards specified by the Principles of Appraisal Practice and the Code of Ethics of the American Appraisal Association. He also describes the components of a typical appraisal report and identifies common valuation errors.

Conclusion

These proceedings present a look at the valuation of closely held companies and inactively traded securities from the perspective of some of the leading practitioners in the field. The presentations offer practicing appraisers, attorneys, business brokers, CPAs, executors, financial and estate planners, business owners, prospective business owners, and other interested parties an introduction to this highly specialized and complex area of finance. It is hoped that the understanding of the practice of business valuation, and the quality of future valuations, will be enhanced through the insights presented here.

The Legal Environment and Its Impact on Valuation

Robert P. Oliver

The legal environment is very important in the valuation of closely held companies because most valuation work is generated by laws. Curiosity rarely motivates the owner of a closely held corporation to hire a business appraiser to value his or her business; rather, valuations are performed when the owner's business or personal affairs collide with a law requiring a valuation. Typically, these laws relate to estate and gift taxes, employee benefits, state dissenters' rights statutes, income taxes, or divorce, not to mention lawsuits between family members or partners.

There are many similarities between the work of an investment analyst and a business-valuation expert: They each need to be well versed in accounting, economics, finance, statistics, and allied disciplines; and they need to be skilled in interviewing management and analyzing companies. There is, however, one major difference in their work: Business-valuation experts cannot stop at fair market value or freely traded value—they must consider additional issues like control premia, marketability discounts, premia for voting power, discounts for nonvoting stock, and oddball legal contrivances like fair value.

Valuations for estate- and gift-tax purposes are an important part of the valuation practices of most closely held corporations. The Internal Revenue Service Appeals Officer Valuation Training Program includes a booklet which states that "experience has shown that problems involving the valuation of closely held securities make up the majority of valuation issues arising in the estate and gift tax fields." The booklet also indicates that the appeals philosophy of the IRS is to settle issues "without controversy, promptly and without litigation" but that in valuation cases, the achievement of that goal is often "more time consuming, difficult and fraught with frustration."[1]

The regulations under the estate- and gift-tax laws provide the definition of fair market value that is used in most valuations: The price at which the

property would change hands between a willing buyer and a willing seller, when the former is not under any compulsion to buy and the latter is not under any compulsion to sell, and both parties have a reasonable knowledge of relevant facts.

The estate- and gift-tax regulations also provide appraisers with what is probably their most important regulatory guideline or legal requirement: Revenue Ruling 59-60. Its importance derives not only from the fact that it is part of the law, but also because it makes sense. Prior to 1953, all examinations of estate- and gift-tax returns were handled in the IRS National Office in Washington, D.C. After 1953, the IRS decentralized that function and issued guidelines to its field officers. In 1959, Revenue Ruling 59-60 was issued, superseding all previous guidelines. In 1965, Revenue Ruling 59-60 was expanded to include closely held stock valuations for income-tax purposes and other tax purposes, as well as business interests of any type and intangible assets for all purposes.

Estate- and Gift-Tax Laws

The valuation of a closely held corporation for estate- and gift-tax purposes must adhere to the requirements of Revenue Ruling 59-60. This ruling provides a good framework for preparing valuations. A concise but reasonably comprehensive document, it places the IRS on record both publicly and internally as an advocate of sound valuation practices accepted by the business-valuation profession, exercised by the investing public, and formalized by the courts. Because it is only a framework, however, it leaves some room for professional judgment.

Revenue Ruling 59-60 provides both general and specific guidelines for valuing closely held companies. It stresses that all relevant factors affecting fair market value must be considered. This ruling states that there is no general formula that is applicable to the many different valuation situations. The emphasis in Revenue Ruling 59-60 is that valuation is a question of fact and that value depends upon the circumstances in each case. Fortunately, it ac-

---

[1] *IRS Valuation Guide for Income, Estate and Gift Taxes.* Federal Estate and Gift Tax Report. Chicago: Commerce Clearing House, Inc. (May 11, 1982.)

knowledges that, although valuation is based upon the relevant facts, these facts must be weighted with elements of common sense, informed judgment, and reasonableness, according to their significance.

Revenue Ruling 59-60 suggests that the prices of actively traded stocks reflect the consensus of investors about the future; therefore, value is essentially a prophecy of the future. One of the best measures of the value of a closely held company is the stock prices of publicly held companies that are engaged in the same or a similar line of business. The use of publicly held companies to derive standards for valuing a closely held company is a basic tool of business valuation.

In addition to these general instructions, Revenue Ruling 59-60 calls for consideration of the following specific factors and discusses each in detail.

1. The nature of the business and the history of the enterprise since its inception.
2. The economic outlook in general and the condition and outlook of the specific industry in particular.
3. The book value of the stock and the financial condition of the business.
4. The earning capacity of the company.
5. The dividend-paying capacity of the company.
6. Whether or not the enterprise has goodwill or other intangible values.
7. Sales of stock and the size of the block of stock to be valued.
8. The market price of stocks of corporations engaged in the same or a similar line of business, having their stocks actively traded in a free and open market, on an exchange, or over the counter.

A sound valuation analysis is a sophisticated interpretation of Revenue Ruling 59-60. By and large, appraisers are comfortable working under the requirements of Revenue Ruling 59-60. It has been a useful guideline for about 30 years.

The Internal Revenue Code not only provides guidelines for how to do an evaluation, it also imposes penalties on appraisers and taxpayers for the undervaluation or overvaluation of assets as outlined in Section 6660. Code Section 6660 provides for an addition to the estate or gift tax of up to 30 percent of the tax ultimately due if the value originally claimed in the estate's tax return is less than 40 percent of the value ultimately determined by a court or in a settlement with the IRS. This is a considerable penalty for undervaluations. The risk exists for both the appraiser and the taxpayer because the law provides for a $1,000 civil penalty imposed on an appraiser if it is demonstrated that the appraiser has

aided or abetted in the undervaluation of the asset. The IRS can also bar an appraiser from participating as an expert in future IRS proceedings concerning the valuation of assets. Similar penalties apply to the overvaluation of assets for charitable-gift and tax-deduction purposes where taxpayers might be motivated to have a higher value to get a higher tax savings.

A landmark case in business valuation, the *Central Trust* case, was decided in 1962, not long after Revenue Ruling 59-60 became law.[2] The opinion deals directly with many basic valuation concepts. The basic facts of this case were as follows.

On various dates in 1954, a stockholder of the Heekin Can Company gave minority-interest blocks of stock to his children. Originally, those shares were valued at $10 per share. On amended returns, however, the shares were valued at $7.50. In auditing the returns, the IRS claimed the value of the stock was $24 per share. At the trial, there were five expert witnesses; the government had two and the taxpayer had three. The taxpayer's witnesses testified to values ranging from $7.88 per share to $11.41 per share. One of the government experts determined a value of $16.00 per share, and the other a value of $22.50 per share. It is interesting to note that the government retained an independent business-valuation expert in addition to its own appraiser. The staff appraiser testified to the highest value per share.

In reviewing the testimony, a court found that the value of the shares was $15.50. In arriving at an opinion, the court is not bound by the testimony of any single expert. It can choose from among the evidence presented in the testimony as it deems appropriate. The *Central Trust* case is important because the judge sorted through the material in a clearly explained and logical manner, which is not always the case. The key conceptual and factual issues considered were the capitalization of earnings or dividends, the use of book value, the importance of prior sales of the stock, the use of comparative companies, and a discount for lack of marketability. These are some of the most basic and important issues faced in valuing every privately held company.

The court indicated that capitalized earnings were the most important factor in the valuation of a manufacturing company. The court also affirmed the notion that earnings should be adjusted for any unusual or nonrecurring items in order to get a measure of ongoing earning power. Significant differences in the expert witnesses' valuations related to

[2]Central Trust Co. v. United States, 305 F.2d 393 (1962).

their definitions of the earnings base. The court required that any trend in earnings be considered. In this case, there was an upward trend, so the court used a weighted average of earnings. The expert witnesses used different valuation dates with respect to the earnings bases. The court asserted that earnings information up to the date of valuation should be used, and it prepared its valuation accordingly.

Some of the experts capitalized a five-year average of dividends to determine an indicated value based on dividends. The court felt strongly that the most weight should be given to the most recent dividend payments in assessing the dividend-paying capacity of the company. The court took into consideration the need to retain funds and to finance anticipated and known future capital expenditures, which is important because the typical private company's most important source of funds is its retained earnings.

The book value of a company is one measure of the company's value. The court agreed that book value should be given consideration in valuation; however, it was not given much weight in the final analysis.

Prior sales of stock are another factor to be considered in determining the value of a closely held company. In this case, there were transactions in the stock during the four years preceding the critical date, all at $7.50 per share. Some of the taxpayer's witnesses gave weight to those prior sales in their determinations of value. The court felt that those witnesses gave too much weight to the prior sales prices, and it was disturbed by the fact that the price had not changed over the four-year period, although the company's circumstances had changed. The court implied that prior sales of a closely held stock could be given some weight in valuation if those prior sales were on an arm's-length basis, and if no substantial changes in the company's basic circumstances occurred between the date of those prior sales and the valuation date.

Perhaps the most important comments made by the court in this landmark case pertain to the use of comparable companies. The court said this method was a sound and well-accepted technique. All but one of the experts utilized comparable companies as a source for valuation multiples. The court stressed that an appraiser should rely on as broad a base of reasonably comparable companies as possible. The IRS staff expert had used the two premier firms in the can industry. The court criticized him for the use of those firms, saying they were not comparable, from an investment viewpoint, to a smaller firm in the industry like Heekin Can.

Today it is accepted that a discount for lack of

marketability should be applied in the valuation of a closely held corporation. In the *Central Trust* case, four of the five experts had applied a discount for lack of marketability, measured by public-offering flotation costs. The court affirmed that a discount for lack of marketability should be applied to closely held stock, and the court relied on flotation costs as a measure of the discount. Today, however, more appraisers look at the discounts seen in private sales of restricted stock in determining the size of the discount for lack of marketability.

The experts applied different weights to the values indicated by the factors of earning power, dividends, book value, and prior sales. The determination of these weights is based on judgment. The court gave some guidance on the use and size of these weights in its valuation conclusion. In this case, the judge used a weight of 50 percent on the earnings factor, 30 percent on the dividend factor, and 20 percent on the book-value factor. No direct weight was given to prior sales. The fact that these weights have been seen many times in valuation work attests to their significance and reasonableness.

The value of $15.50 determined by the judge in the *Central Trust* case was the average of the five values presented by the experts. Although I believe this was more a coincidence than a goal, it was common for courts to appear to arrive at conclusions that "split the difference." The taxpayer comes in low, the IRS comes in high, and the judge appears to split it down the middle.

In 1980, the tax courts put the taxpayers and the IRS on notice. The policy put in place has had implications for valuation work and for taxpayers. In several court cases the judges specifically stated that they will not simply compromise between the two values, but instead will decide on the merits of the valuation case presented. The first case espousing this doctrine was the Buffalo Tool and Die Manufacturing Company, Inc. v. Commissioner, 74 TC 441 (1980), a case that involved the valuation of the assets of a company. In that case, the judge stated:

> Indeed, each of the parties should keep in mind that, in the final analysis, the Court may find the evidence of valuation by one of the parties sufficiently more convincing than that of the other party, so that the final result will produce a significant financial defeat for one or the other rather than a middle-of-the-road compromise, which we suspect each of the parties expects the Court to reach. If the parties insist on our valuing any or all of the assets, we will.

The same theme was echoed in the *Sirloin Stockade* case, in which the judge referred to the *Buffalo Tool* case and said: "The overtones of respondent's presentation suggest that he counted on the fact that we would find some middle ground between the values of $5.00 and $0.508 per share of Sirloin's common stock. If that was his objective, he has missed his mark." In other words, the judge did not split the difference.[3]

Another good example of the impact of the legal environment on business valuation occurred in 1981 with Revenue Ruling 81-253, which was soon followed by a landmark case, the *Bright* case.[4] In issuing Revenue Ruling 81-253, the IRS was attempting to impose a higher cost on the transfer of ownership in family companies. Generally, if a father with control of a company made a gift of a minority stock interest to a child, that gift would be valued on the basis of a discounted minority interest. This had been and continues to be an accepted practice. In the revenue ruling, the IRS attempted to assert that an ownership transfer, where a family has control of a company, should be valued on a controlling-interest basis. In other words, a gift of 10 percent of the stock of a company should be valued as 10 percent of the enterprise or controlling-interest-basis value of the company and not at the lower minority-interest basis. If Revenue Ruling 81-253 had prevailed, the cost of ownership transfer would have risen considerably, and appraisers would have been doing more controlling-interest valuations than minority-interest valuations.

In every court case where this matter has been an issue, Revenue Ruling 81-253 and the IRS have lost. The first case in which the government was defeated on this issue was the *Bright* case. Mrs. Bright, the decedent, and her husband owned 55 percent of several Texas corporations. The government stated that Mrs. Bright's interest should be valued as one-half of a 55 percent controlling-interest block. In Texas, however, the block could be split, and the estate had no way to prevent the 55-percent block from becoming two 27.5-percent minority-interest blocks. The court rejected the government's control arguments and implicitly rejected Revenue Ruling 81-253. According to the court, the willing buyer and the willing seller referred to in the definition of fair market value are hypothetical, unallied, and independent buyers and sellers. It cannot be assumed that a buyer is a family member or, further, that assumptions can be made about the motivations, attitudes, or behavior of family members. For example, it cannot be assumed that family members would act in concert, or even that they would be willing to buy the stock.

[3]Sirloin Stockade, Inc. v. Commissioner, 40 TCM 928 (1980).

[4]The Estate of Bright v. United States, 658 F.2d 999 (1981).

A word of caution is in order, however, because Revenue Ruling 81-253 is still on the books and a recent technical advice memorandum has, under a different fact set, raised the control issue again.

ESOP Guidelines

There have been only a few guidelines in the Employee Stock Ownership Plan (ESOP) valuation area in the past. In the Employee Retirement Income Security Act (ERISA) in 1974, Congress directed the Department of Labor to promulgate adequate-consideration regulations pertaining to the valuation of closely held stock for ESOP purposes. After a 14-year delay on the part of the Department of Labor, proposed adequate-consideration regulations were issued in May 1988. During that 14-year period, the business-valuation profession struggled with many difficult ESOP valuation issues. Although the legal and business-valuation professions have worked at reasonable solutions to some of these difficult issues, problems remain.

Court cases are important guidelines, but there have been relatively few published cases in the ESOP valuation field. In my opinion, the landmark case in the field is the *U.S. News & World Report* case, not only because of the issues involved, but also because almost every prominent player in the business valuation field was either working on or was asked to work on the case.[5]

The *U. S. News & World Report* case involved a lawsuit initiated by a group of employees who retired from the company saying they received too low a price for their stock when they were paid out of the company's profit-sharing plan. Technically, the issues did not involve an ESOP, because it was a profit-sharing plan, but the valuation issues are really the same. Some of the employees also owned stock under a stock bonus plan. The corporate stock had been in employee benefit plans since 1962, and an independent, nationally known appraisal firm had valued the stock regularly for the profit-sharing plan. By 1981, the stock was valued at $470 per share. In 1984, the company was sold for $2,842 per share, more than five times the last appraised value. Although the profit-sharing plan had started with a minority-interest block of stock, the holdings of the plan by the 1970s constituted a majority of the outstanding shares of the company. The stock was voted by a voting trust.

[5]Charles S. Foltz, et al., U. S. News & World Report, Inc., et al., and Davis B. Richardson, et al., v. U. S. News & World Report, Inc., et. al. U. S. District Court, District of Columbia, Civil Actions No. 84-0447 and 85-2195, June 22, 1987.

One reason for the large difference between the 1981 appraised value and the eventual sale price of the company was the valuable real estate owned by the company in Washington, D.C. For most of the period under review, the company had no plans to develop that real estate, although in the early 1980s some preliminary plans were underway. The judge had to deal with some of the most difficult ESOP valuation issues in preparing his opinion.

The issue of valuation on a controlling-interest basis versus a minority-interest basis was perhaps the key issue in this case. All of the appraisals for plan purposes had valued the stock on a minority-interest basis. The employee plaintiffs argued that the stock should have been valued on a controlling-interest basis. As we know, a controlling-interest owner can generally realize the value of the underlying assets of the company, and a minority-interest investor cannot. In resolving the control- versus minority-interest issue, the court reached a conclusion that is consistent with a reasonable valuation practice. The court observed that just because the number of plan shares constituted numerical control of the company, it did not follow that any one employee should receive his *pro rata* share of a controlling interest. The court further observed that because the shares were held in a voting trust, the appraised values justifiably could have been lower. The most telling comment of the court on this control- versus minority-interest issue, in the context of this legal environment topic, is that there existed no legal, regulatory, or judicial authority for the use of a control value. The court concluded that the use of a minority-interest valuation was reasonable. The Department of Labor had not issued guidelines in this area at the time of the trial and still has not.

Another issue in the ESOP area is the size of the discount for lack of marketability. Unlike other cases where a put option is in place, U.S News had no obligation to buy the shares back; it only had an option to call the shares. Considering this and other factors, the appraisers applied a 10 percent discount for lack of marketability in valuing the stock. In reviewing the facts of the case, the court concluded that a 10 percent discount was perfectly reasonable.

The major reason for the differences in the appraised value and the eventual sale price was the value of Washington, D.C. real estate. The court confirmed the concept that, in the valuation of the stock of a company on a minority-interest basis, earnings should be given primary consideration. Because a minority-interest shareholder cannot access those underlying assets, in the absence of a plan to realize the values of those underlying assets they should be given less weight in valuing the stock. In fact, the court stated that any realizable value of the real estate should be attributed to the common stock only if it is evident that the controlling interest had a firm and clear intent to dispose of the real estate within a very short or reasonable period of time. This was not the factual matter of the case.

Fair Value

Another area where the law has a direct impact on valuation practice is with respect to the concept of fair value. Under common law a minority shareholder can block the sale or merger of a company. Accordingly, to protect majority owners from arbitrary minority owners, states have passed laws that permit mergers to be ratified by less than 100 percent of the shares. Typically, a vote of up to two-thirds of the outstanding shares is required to approve a merger. Fair value is a creation of state laws giving minority shareholders a remedy for their dissent to a corporate merger approved by majority shareholders. If you dissent to a merger, your relief or remedy is the determination of fair value of your stock.

The term "fair value" is used in only 12 states. Nineteen states reference this concept as fair value exclusive of any element of value arising from the expectation or accomplishment of the corporate transaction, or similar language. The statutes differ. For example, some states use the term "fair cash value" and others use "fair value." There is not a lot of guidance for the definition of fair value in these laws. One has to look to the court decisions in each jurisdiction to see what factors are considered in the determination of fair value.

Many states—but not all—have looked to Delaware cases for guidance. Historically, in Delaware, fair value has been determined by the use of a weighted average, with varying weights given to the factors of investment value, market value, and net asset value. More recently, cases have indicated that fair value may equal enterprise value or sale/merger value.

A good illustration of this recent development is the *Cavalier Oil* case.[6] It involved appraisal demands by a dissenting minority shareholder, Mr. Harnett, in separate mergers of two related closely held companies. One of these companies was engaged in managing rental houses owned by various investment partnerships that had the same corporate general partner. The other company was engaged in the

[6]Cavalier Oil Corporation v. Harnett, Del. Ch. Civil Action Nos. 7959, 7960, 7967, 7968 (1988).

origination, sale, and servicing of mortgages for these houses.

In arriving at their determination of fair value, the company's experts first valued each corporation on an enterprise basis and then reduced these values by 28 percent to reflect the minority-interest status of Harnett's shares. This minority-interest value was then discounted 40 percent for lack of marketability. The combined discount was 55 percent from the enterprise value and represented a minority-interest fair market value for closely held stock.

Before determining the fair value of Harnett's stock in each company, the court considered the meaning of "fair value" under Section 262 of Delaware corporation law. Specifically, it addressed the question: Does this section permit the appraised value of a corporation to be discounted to reflect the fact that the dissenting shareholder's stock reprsents a minority interest and is not readily marketable?

The court rejected the application of a minority-interest discount because Delaware law requires an appraisal of the corporation as an entity and a going concern. The court then gives the dissenter his proportionate interest in this overall fair value. The objective is not to value the dissenters' specific stock interest in the corporation as such; therefore, the size of his interest is immaterial except to determine his fraction of the total company value.

The court also rejected the application of a discount for lack of marketability for the same reason: Delaware law requires a valuation of the entire corporation as a going concern, not a valuation of the specific stock owned by the dissenting shareholder. So, it appears as though the judge concluded that fair value was equal to enterprise value.

The *Cavalier Oil* case is also of interest because of the appraisal methods employed by both sides. Harnett's appraiser relied exclusively on discounted-cash-flow (DCF) analysis to value each company. The companies' appraisers also relied on DCF analysis, but the results were averaged with other appraisals—one based on asset values, in the case of the mortgage company, and one based on comparable companies, in the case of the management company.

The experts chose very similar discount rates for their valuations, but their projections of future revenues, expenses, and dividends were radically different. As a result, Harnett's valuation of the mortgage company stock was more than 10 times the company's figure, and his valuation of the management company stock was two times greater than the company's figure. The court accepted the methodology of Harnett's mortgage company appraisal, but changed some of the factual assumptions to arrive at a lower valuation of its own. The court also accepted Harnett's specific appraisal of the management company. In so doing, it rejected the company's argument that a separate comparable-company analysis was required because the comparable-company method is more accurate than the DCF method. The court noted that both methods require the exercise of expert judgment: "The relevant ratios for the comparable companies may be based upon historical fact, but the threshold determination of which companies are 'comparable' is highly judgmental. So is the determination of what multiples are appropriate for the company being appraised."

The court rejected the related argument that a comparable-company analysis was required to establish the validity of the earnings multiplier and discount factors used in a DCF analysis. It held that the reasonableness of these factors could be established by other evidence. One expert used a range of 14 to 20 percent, and the other side used a range of 20 to 25 percent; the judge used 20 percent.

This case is interesting for still another reason. It shows what can happen when a judge does not accept the valuations presented by the parties and does his own. When Harnett's appraiser valued the mortgage company, he projected its earnings for five years. To arrive at a terminal value, he then assumed the company would go public early in the sixth year and that the underwriters would price its stock at 12 times the projected fifth-year earnings. The judge liked the price/earnings (P/E) ratio of 12 but felt the earnings base selected by the appraiser produced too high a terminal value. Therefore, he substituted what he considered a more realistic earnings figure, which was an average of the company's historical earnings for the three years preceding the appraisal date. He multiplied that by 12 to get a terminal value.

The judge did not seem concerned by the fact that the use of a public-offering P/E ratio would cause the terminal value to reflect a minority-interest discount—something he had just decided was improper. Also, the judge's opinion failed to make clear how the validity of a public-offering P/E ratio could be established for use in connection with a DCF analysis without any examination of comparable companies—something else he had disapproved.

The Capital Asset Pricing Model

The *Northern Trust* case, the first valuation case involving the use of the capital asset pricing model (CAPM), was decided in 1986.[7]

[7]The Northern Trust Company v. Commissioner, 87 TC No. 349 (1986).

The *Northern Trust* case involved a valuation of the voting and nonvoting common stocks of Curran Contracting Company, which was engaged in the asphalt-paving and railroad-equipment businesses and held additional nonoperating assets. The taxpayer's expert valued the stocks first by the comparable-company method, using a separate group of similar publicly held companies for each of Curran's principal lines of business. This expert also prepared a second valuation using the discounted-cash-flow method. He determined the proper discount rate to apply to the cash-flow and residual-value projections by using the CAPM to compute Curran's cost of equity capital. To obtain a beta, he utilized samples of common stocks of publicly held companies engaged in the construction and railroad supply businesses.

The IRS expert used only the comparable-company method. In applying this, he selected a group of publicly held companies that had a return on equity, sales volume, and debt/equity ratio similar to Curran's. He did not consider the specific type of business in which each of these companies was engaged.

The court rejected the taxpayer's comparable-company valuation because the publicly held companies selected by the expert were not engaged in sufficiently comparable businesses. The court also rejected the IRS's comparable-company valuation, noting that the financial measures used to select the publicly held companies were meaningless without considering the businesses in which these companies were engaged.

One of the most significant factors in this case is the endorsement of the CAPM. The court accepted the taxpayer's approach, which utilized both the DCF model and the CAPM, concluding that it was consistent with the requirements of Revenue Ruling 59-60. The court made adjustments to the taxpayer's analysis, however, and applied different minority-interest and lack-of-marketability discounts, to arrive at its own valuation. An equal value per share was then allocated to the two types of common stock.

One thing is troublesome about this case. It seems inconsistent for the court to find that the publicly held companies selected by the taxpayer's expert were too dissimilar for a comparable-company valuation approach, but similar enough to measure beta for a DCF or CAPM valuation.

The Choice of Comparable Companies

The search for and choice of comparative companies is a key element in business valuation. In the *Hall*

case, this valuation issue is addressed directly.[8]

This case involved an estate-tax deficiency of over $200 million that was primarily attributable to the valuation of the decedent's stock in Hallmark Cards, Incorporated. As seen in many other cases, the valuation experts for the estate and the IRS arrived at valuation results that were extremely far apart, with the estate at $1.79 per share and the IRS at $4.40 per share.

The stockholders of Hallmark Cards had developed a formula for valuing the company stock. They placed numerous restrictions on the Hallmark stock and used a formula to establish adjusted book value as the sales price. The formula added a goodwill premium to book value per share, with the goodwill premium based on a multiple of five times five-year average earnings per share. A small premium was added to two of the classes of stock for their voting and dividend preferences, and a discount was subtracted from the third class because of its lack of vote and dividend preferences. The Hall estate relied on this formula in arriving at $1.79 per share for estate-tax purposes.

At the trial, the experts for both sides agreed that there was only one really good comparable company—American Greetings Corporation. One of the experts retained by the estate also used a group of publicly owned firms that were, like Hallmark, producers of consumer products and that were leaders in their industry. They chose the following additional companies: A. T. Cross (Cross pens), Avon (cosmetics), Coca-Cola (soft drinks), Lenox (fine china), and Papercraft (giftware). These companies also had financial characteristics similar to Hallmark. The expert then applied Hallmark's formula to the financial data of the comparable companies over a period of 10 years and compared the resulting formula values, after a discount for lack of marketability, to the actual stock prices of the comparable companies. By and large, the prices based on the formula computations fell within the range of the actual high and low stock prices of the publicly held companies. The expert concluded that the Hallmark formula provided a reasonable estimate of fair market value and opined that the formula value equaled fair market value at the date of the death of Joyce Hall.

The second expert for the estate used American Greetings and some others for a total of 15 companies, all of which were industry leaders with good financial records. Hallmark was compared with each of the companies to develop an appropriate P/E

---

[8]The Estate of Joyce C. Hall v. Commissioner, 92 TC No. 19 (1989).

ratio. The second expert applied a 36 percent discount for lack of marketability and derived a value somewhat higher than Hallmark's formula price. The restrictions on the stock, however, essentially gave the corporation a right of first refusal at the formula price. The second expert did not believe an investor would sue to have the restrictions removed and concluded that the restrictions and formula price set a maximum price for the shares. The expert then discounted the formula price to reflect the fact that sellers would get long-term notes with a below-market interest rate.

The expert hired by the IRS relied on only one comparable company, American Greetings. The IRS argued that it was simply wrong, as a matter of law, to look beyond the one publicly held greeting card company, even though Revenue Ruling 59-60 calls for the use of publicly held companies engaged in the same or similar line of business and these words appeared in the IRS expert's report.

The court put more weight on the word "similar" than the word "same," and concluded that other companies could be used. It stated that "it was inconceivable to us that a potential buyer of Hallmark stock would consider only one comparable company—American Greetings."

Conclusion

As the foregoing examples illustrate, the legal environment has a tremendous impact on the valuation of closely held companies. Laws create the need for business-valuation services and play a major role in how valuations are done.

Question and Answer Session

Question: Is Revenue Ruling 59-60 outdated?

Oliver: No. Discounted-cash-flow techniques are being used more often, but they have not made Revenue Ruling 59-60 outdated. Furthermore, there are still problems with DCF techniques. For example, in the *Cavalier Oil* case, one expert came up with a value 10 times greater than the other side's—just because he used different assumptions as to the growth of the firm in the DCF model.

Pratt: Revenue Ruling 59-60 has stood the test of time. Here we are 30 years later, and virtually everybody in the appraisal profession still refers to it. Although it was written for federal estate-tax valuation purposes, it is widely referred to for other purposes as well, and nothing in it refutes the notion of using discounted-cash-flow analysis. In fact, the ruling specifically says that an appraisal is a prophecy—which is essentially what DCF analysis is. So, in effect, it endorses DCF analysis.

Question: Does the tax code ever specify fair value rather than fair market value?

Oliver: No, not to my knowledge. Fair value is typically the remedy under the dissenters' rights statutes in various states.

Pratt: Fair market value is the standard of value in all tax situations, not only for federal taxes but also for states that have inheritance taxes. Fair value is the standard in most of the states—not all 50—for dissenting stockholders rights. The various states interpret fair value differently, however.

Question: How are voting-trust securities valued?

Oliver: Because the owner of the shares does not vote the shares directly, the owner of the shares voted by a voting trust is in a less-advantageous position than the owner of other voting stocks. Therefore, the value will be less than the value of voting stock.

Pratt: In the *U.S. News* case, one side tried to argue that the profit-sharing plan's shares should be valued at a premium because they were in a voting trust. The judge very vehemently said that an appraiser may take a discount when shares are in a voting trust, but the appraiser may not take a pre-mium. That position has been consistent throughout the case law.

Question: If you have a single shareholder in a thinly traded public company with 48 percent ownership, can he expect a greater value for his shares than the other minority shareholders?

Oliver: If the valuation issue was in an estate context, there might be some justification for a discount from the thinly traded price. On the other hand, if the single shareholder wanted to sell his block of stock, there could be some premium attached to that. More importantly, though, it would have to be determined if the thinly traded price was representative of fair market value. Because of the lack of trading activity, the price could be meaningless as a measure of fair market value.

Question: Is there a premium on owning 100 percent versus 97 percent of the stock of a company?

Pratt: Normally that type of situation arises in a squeeze-out merger; usually, fair-value case law will provide guidance on this question. One must carefully consider the case law in the individual state because it varies from one state to another.

Question: Can subsequent events be used in valuations? In other words, if the valuation date is 1986 and you are testifying in 1989, can the results of the intervening three years be used in the case?

Oliver: Normally, no. But two recent estate-tax cases relate to this issue. These cases involved valuing a company after the key man—the driving force of the company—died. The cases went to trial several years after the men died. The evidence presented included the earnings of these companies subsequent to the dates of death. In both cases, the company's earnings had deteriorated significantly, which supported the argument that these were, in-fact, key employees. Substantial key-man discounts were allowed by the court.

Pratt: Otherwise, it is extremely rare for subsequent events to be given weight, and the thread of the case law, for the most part, is very consistent in not allowing any consideration to subsequent events.

Market Approach to Valuation

James G. Wolf, CFA

The market approach involves valuing a company based on the market valuation of similar publicly held companies. It is typically a "top-down" type of analysis: It begins at the broadest level and progresses to the company-specific level. In this presentation, I will outline the major steps involved in the market approach to valuing a closely held company and provide examples by using a case study format.

Analysis of the Economy

The first step in a market approach is to analyze the economic environment. An analysis of the economy is the basis for evaluating the industry and the companies within the industry.

The analysis of the economy should include an examination of gross national product, industrial production, interest rates, inflation trends, and expectations of future growth. Expectations, however, do not always materialize. For example, most analysts have been predicting a recession during the 1980s, but 1989 is nearly over and there is still no recession (although there appears to be a consensus that there has been a moderate slow-down).

Analysis of the Industry

The second step in a market approach is to conduct an in-depth analysis of the subject company's industry. This analysis should include an evaluation of the the industry's relation to the economy and the competitive environment of companies within the industry. At the most general level, it is important to consider where the industry is in its life cycle and the relation of the industry to economic cycles. The amount of industry regulation, the likelihood of changes in regulation, and the impact of regulation on the firm should also be considered.

The competitive advantages of companies within the industry must be analyzed and understood. For example, to determine a company's potential for profit, one might use the framework outlined by Michael Porter in his book, *Competitive Strategy* (1980). This framework entails evaluating barriers to entry, substitute products, bargaining power of suppliers, bargaining power of buyers, and rivalry among existing competitors. These considerations are especially important in high-tech, highly competitive, price-sensitive industries. One should also consider whether the business is in an oligopoly, a monopoly, or a very competitive industry. The answer will impact various margin and pricing trends—and, of course, value.

The relative competitive advantages of companies may be ascertained by looking at their functional activities—for example, production costs and methods, marketing, distribution, and human resources. These are especially important when one is valuing a business plan; that is, valuing a company that has no existence other than a document stating what the company plans to do after initial funds are raised. Such a company may have technologies, various intangibles, human resources, and so forth, but it is always difficult to value them.

One should analyze the sensitivity of the industry to other forces. Is the demand for this industry's products increasing or decreasing? What is the industry sensitive to—changes in raw-material prices, costs of labor, union strikes? What is the nature of the supply of output within the industry? Pricing and growth are key determinants of value.

Information is vital to the valuation business. The major sources of information on industries are trade association publications, U.S. Industrial Outlook, and ValueLine Investment Survey. Trade associations are an excellent source of information in terms of statistics, financial information, pricing trends, and competitive environment.

Analysis of the Subject Company

The third step in the process is to analyze the subject company. This includes an in-depth analysis of the firm's competitive and financial position. As mentioned, the various industry segments served by the firm must be analyzed in terms of their product classes, types of buyers, distribution channels, and geographic markets. The functions of the firm also must be analyzed and understood—for example, production, marketing, distribution, and management. During a visit to the company, it is important to take a tour of the plant and conduct in-depth interviews with the key managers. A plant tour can provide insight into the efficiency of the manufacturing operation and the need for future capital expenditures.

Examination of the subject company requires a thorough review of every aspect of the business. This includes looking at how much the company has been spending on research and development to determine whether those efforts have been effective; looking at sales over a period of time—not only by dollar volume, but also by unit volume—and trying to understand the trends; and analyzing the sales and profitability of the various product classes to better understand overall company sales and profitability, both historically and in the future. If the company is losing sales of a product that generates a high percentage of its profits, the valuation may not be as high as the valuation based on the income statements for the past 12 months. The overall management team—its style, compensation, and experience—is another important consideration. In particular, it is critical to determine whether the company has a strategic plan that everyone understands and is working to implement.

An analysis of the competition and the company's competitive strategy is crucial. There are several key questions one must ask to gain an understanding of the company.

- Is the company following a strategy for the future (whether it has been committed to writing and followed, or just implied)?
- Is the company a low-cost producer in its industry?
- Is the company a niche competitor that is trying to differentiate itself in terms of products, sales methods, or customers?
- Is competition increasing or decreasing?
- Is the company depending on one product or one market?
- Is it a leader or a follower?
- What has been the history of price increases and introduction of new models or products?
- Why is this company successful? (Each company has a reason for its success; it may be totally different for one firm than a similar company in the same industry.)

Selection of Comparable Companies

The fourth step in the market approach to valuation is to select a set of similar or comparable publicly traded companies (or those that have been acquired).

Once adjustments are made to put the subject company on the same basis as the comparable companies, one may use the market's valuation of the comparable companies as a proxy for the valuation of the subject company.

The comparable companies are selected to match as closely as possible the industry and the function of the subject firm. To identify comparable companies, consideration is given to SIC codes, business functions, financial characteristics, market characteristics, and any unique issues that may be involved. Sometimes it is hard to find comparable companies. Many companies have multiple lines of business that are radically different—or are more integrated—than the subject's. Companies have different geographic markets: Some companies are international in scope, others are regional. Because one must make subjective judgments about which companies to use, one must understand the true nature of the subject company and each comparable.

The choice of comparable companies will also be affected by whether one is valuing a minority interest or the entire company. A detailed review of potential comparable companies must be made to learn whether any of those companies should be eliminated from the selection. Typically, some comparables must be discarded because of general functional differences or because financial results are not comparable (for example, loss of money, recapitalization, material acquisitions, or divestitures). Some companies are clearly not comparable: Obviously one would not want to use the manufacturer of a product for the housing industry as a comparable for the manufacturer of a product in the high-tech industry.

Case Study: To illustrate the market approach to valuation, we will value a company in the roofing materials industry. To do a market valuation of the subject company, the analyst must first perform an analysis of the economy, the industry, and the subject company. The next step is to select a set of comparable companies. In this case, four companies (A, B, C, and D) are chosen as comparables. The companies are similar to the subject company in terms of their basic businesses, geographic markets, and so forth. Three of them (companies A, B, and D) have a December fiscal year, company C has a June fiscal year, and the subject company has an October fiscal year. The analysis is for 1989.

Once the comparable companies have been selected, a detailed analysis of their lines of business is conducted. In many cases, the subject company will not have a set of exactly comparable publicly traded firms. In this situation, one analyzes the potential comparable companies to see whether their underlying products are the same, whether their manufacturing processes or their consumers are similar, and so forth. One must also look at how similar the comparable companies are in their financial characteristics—for example, sales, assets, leverage, liquidity, utilization of assets, and profitability. One must look at both the size of these factors and the rates of growth, both historically and prospectively.

The marketability of a company's stock is an important consideration in a minority-interest calculation. The number of publicly traded companies with sales of $5 million to $10 million is amazing, but those shares may not always be marketable. The size of the last trade relative to the typical trade is important: large blocks typically have a much greater impact on these stocks than on a company listed on the New York Stock Exchange or the American Stock Exchange. As the following example will illustrate, it is important to determine exactly how marketable a company's stock really is.

> **Example**. The quoted price on a small company is $1.00. A call to the market maker reveals that the bid is $0.50 and the ask is $1.00 and that the last transaction was several months ago. A call to the company reveals that most trades are not arms-length transactions. Clearly, the $1.00 price is not a sure bet.

Financial Analysis of the Subject and Comparable Companies

The historical income statements and balance sheets of the subject and the comparable companies are used to identify the impact on value of differences between them. The process of analyzing comparable companies involves identifying similarities and differences and making adjustments to put the companies on a comparable basis. The types of adjustments will differ depending on whether the valuation is for a controlling interest or a minority interest. A minority interest has no control over realizing asset values, changing depreciation methods, terminating a pension fund, and so forth; therefore, fewer adjustments will be done.

Adjustments must be made for companies that use different inventory-valuation methods. For comparisons of cash flows to be relevant, the companies must be on the same inventory basis—for example, LIFO (last in, first out) or FIFO (first in, first out). Also, if the companies are using LIFO, the analyst must look at the materiality of the LIFO reserve, especially if an enterprise valuation is being performed.

One may also need to adjust for nontangible assets and off-balance-sheet financings to make the firms comparable. The materiality of goodwill and related amortization expenses, as well as the economic impact of leases, must be evaluated. The effect on earnings of different lease accounting methods may be significant.

Other considerations are capitalized interest, different depreciation methods, and pension fund issues. The sale of divisions or assets and any general restructuring are important considerations in analyzing publicly traded companies over time. When something happens that impacts the financial statement, the analysis must be adjusted accordingly.

The components of capital structure must be considered and understood. The effects of outstanding issues of preferred stock, warrants, options, and convertible debt must be analyzed. Stock splits should also be taken into account.

There are some basic adjustments to financial statements of closely held companies that should always be considered. The adjustments that follow are not necessarily made if one is valuing a minority interest, because a minority owner does not have the ability to control the company's affairs. These adjustments are more typical of valuations of a controlling interest: adjustments for the effects of owners' and officers' compensation; significant nonoperating assets—for example, cash, real estate, and pension funds; large loans to and from officers and their relatives; other related-party transactions; less-than-market-value leases; and contingent liabilities. The statistics of comparable companies and general industry statistics may be used to identify normal practices. Adjustments to the financial statements provide the analyst with a normalized income statement and balance sheet, which should reflect how a typical third-party owner would operate the company. The adjusted financial statements are the basis for the market valuation.

Case Study: Once the comparable companies have been selected, the analyst must do a financial analysis of the companies. A summary of the financial analysis illustrated in this case study is presented in the Appendix, Tables 1 through 7. **Table 1** shows the income statement analysis for the four companies relative to the subject company. (Data for all tables was compiled from the companies' 10-K, 10-Q, and annual reports.) On the basis of income statement comparisons, companies A, C, and D are very similar to the subject company, as shown by the percentage of earnings before depreciation, interest, and taxes. Looking at the gross profit margin, it appears that the subject company (64.7 percent) is not comparable to the other companies (33.2 percent average). The difference is explained by the fact that the subject company uses a different method to report cost of goods sold. Looking at the operating margin, which excludes other income, we see that companies A and D are most comparable.

Table 2 shows the comparative balance sheet analysis. The subject company has very high cash equivalents; this suggests that some adjustments may have to be made to the cash accounts. Company B shows a lot of cash (relatively speaking), but upon further analysis it turns out that company B has a relatively low asset base—so the cash-equivalents ratio may not be truly reflective of excess cash. All of the companies have been put on an FIFO basis.

It is interesting to note the relative use of leverage, although the amount of leverage is not very important because the analysis is on an enterprise basis. Of the comparable companies, company A has the lowest amount of long-term debt, and company C has the highest. The amount of long-term debt for companies B and D is closer to the industry's average, although it is still greater than the subject company's. Also, the fact that company A has preferred stock must be considered.

The historical analysis of companies typically involves five to ten years of data. This is supplemented by a current-period analysis, which normally covers the most recent 12 months. In doing a trailing 12-month analysis, one must be aware of differences in seasonality between the companies. Differences in fiscal-year reporting periods should also be noted. If the subject company uses a December fiscal year and the other companies use a June fiscal year, comparisons may be misleading.

Ratio analysis is an important part of the financial analysis. It is important to look at trends in such ratios as accounts receivable outstanding, inventory turnover, sales per employee, debt to total capital, debt to equity, return on assets, return on equity, and liquidity.

Case Study: Table 3 shows the ratio analysis. Companies B and D have the closest sales level to the subject, whereas company A's assets-to-equity and debt-to-equity ratios are more similar. The interest-coverage ratio is not reported for the subject because it has little long-term debt outstanding. Overall, the comparables are similar to the subject. For example, the inventory-turnover ratios for companies A, C, and D are similar to the subject's.

One of the cornerstones of ratio analysis is the DuPont analysis, because it focuses the analyst's attention on key aspects of a company's performance by breaking down the return-on-equity ratio into several component ratios. Table 4 shows the components of the return-on-equity analysis for the past three years using the DuPont formula.

Return-on-equity and growth expectations are important inputs to the market approach. Table 5 presents a growth-rate analysis. Both the subject and company A have low to negative sales growth; all of the companies are experiencing negative EBIT growth.

One should also make the standard comparisons of sales and profit trends. This may be done by comparing such things as net income, earnings before interest and taxes (EBIT), or operating profits before depreciation, amortization, and operating leverage. For some closely held companies it is easy to separate the fixed costs from the variable costs. For other companies, this is not possible.

Analysis of Multiples

The analysis of the subject and comparable companies results in a set of adjustments that puts them on a consistent basis. The next step is to determine an appropriate multiple for these companies. There are several approaches. One is to use price/earnings (P/E) multiples. Several definitions of earnings are used, including operating income, income before depreciation and noncash expenditures, and fully diluted earnings. Other methods use price to cash flow, price to sales, and price to book value of common equity. Also, total invested capital to each cash item should be considered. The multiples are as follows:

- Price (Market Value) to Cash Flow
- Price (Market Value) to Earnings
- Price (Market Value) to EBIT
- Price (Market Value) to EBDIT
- Price (Market Value) to Sales
- Price (Market Value) to Book Value.

One should use the total invested capital as the numerator for each of these ratios. In addition, three- and five-year averages may be used. Alternatively, one could use a dividend-capitalization approach using the well-known dividend discount model.

In addition to choosing the appropriate multiple, one must choose the period of earnings or cash flow to use. Typically, the latest 12 months' earnings or cash flow are used. There are several considerations in choosing the appropriate time period; for example, the relation between the prior period's earnings and normalized post and future earnings, and the possible deviations in the trend of earnings from expected future earnings. If available, multiples that reflect estimates of the next 12 months' results should be used to factor growth into the analysis.

If the comparable companies do not have acceptable earnings or cash-flow figures, another valuation method must be used, such as an asset approach or a discounted-future-cash-flow approach.

Case Study: **Table 6** provides comparative-market and earnings-per-share data. **Table 7** presents an analysis of valuation multiples based on trailing 12-month earnings. Because this was a full-control or enterprise value, more consideration was given to the total-invested-capital multiples, in particular total invested capital to EBDIT, total invested capital to cash flow, total market capital (TMC) to debt-free cash flow, price to cash flow, and price to EBDIT.

A review of the multiples indicates some problems. It turns out that companies A and D had sold some divisions. When the sales are taken into consideration, the multiples are materially different than they are without this adjustment. In this case, I decided to drop two of the potential comparables after completing the financial analysis. I dropped company B because it was going out of business. In fact, company D was putting company B out of business. I dropped company C because it was a very large company relative to the other ones; it had the highest operating profits and a high return on equity.

Conclusion: The Valuation

The final step in the process is to decide where the subject company fits relative to the comparable companies. Once this is done, a range of relevant multiples may be applied to the subject company's base to determine its value.

Case Study: I valued the company at $9 million.

Appendix

TABLE 1. Market Approach: Comparative Income Statement Analysis (Adjusted)

	Company A	Company B	Company C	Company D	Subject Company
Inventory method	LIFO	LIFO	LIFO	FIFO	LIFO
Sales	100.0%	100.0%	100.0%	100.0%	100.0%
Adjusted COGS (FIFO)	77.0%	45.2%	74.6%	70.3%	35.3%
Gross profit	23.0%	54.8%	25.4%	29.7%	64.7%
Operating expenses	17.7%	53.9%	18.1%	25.1%	59.7%
Operating margin	5.3%	0.9%	7.3%	4.6%	5.0%
Other income	0.2%	1.0%	0.3%	0.4%	2.4%
Other expenses	0.0%	0.2%	0.0%	0.0%	0.0%
Adjusted	-1.3%	0.0%	0.0%	1.9%	0.0%
EBDIT	4.6%	1.7%	7.5%	6.9%	7.4%
Depreciation and amortization	2.2%	2.1%	4.2%	4.2%	3.4%
EBIT	2.4%	-0.4%	3.3%	2.8%	4.0%
Gross interest expenses	1.8%	1.4%	2.1%	1.6%	0.0%
Earnings before taxes	0.6%	-1.7%	1.2%	1.2%	4.0%
Taxes	0.3%	-0.8%	0.3%	0.5%	1.1%
Adjusted net income before extraordinary items	0.3%	-0.9%	0.9%	0.7%	2.8%
Extraordinary items	5.9%	-0.7%	0.0%	-3.2%	0.8%
Tax rate	46.2%	45.9%	25.8%	38.7%	28.9%

Source: The author, James G. Wolf, is the source of all tables in this presentation.

TABLE 2. Market Approach: Comparative Balance Sheet Analysis (Adjusted)

	Company A	Company B	Company C	Company D	Subject Company
Cash equivalent	0.2%	7.3%	2.8%	0.3%	31.5%
Accounts receivable	37.2%	9.5%	21.3%	27.4%	28.1%
Adjusted inventory (FIFO)	27.2%	41.6%	21.2%	24.9%	10.1%
Other current assets	1.0%	6.2%	3.8%	6.3%	4.0%
Total current assets	65.5%	64.6%	49.1%	58.8%	73.6%
Net PP&E	31.1%	22.8%	46.0%	40.2%	24.3%
Other assets	3.4%	12.6%	4.9%	1.0%	2.1%
Total assets	100.0%	100.0%	100.0%	100.0%	100.0%
Accounts payable	25.4%	6.9%	9.2%	11.3%	8.8%
Current long-term debt	0.5%	0.4%	0.9%	1.4%	0.0%
Other current liabilities	2.6%	45.4%	10.9%	5.2%	5.1%
Total current liabilities	28.5%	52.7%	20.9%	17.9%	13.9%
Total long-term debt	9.2%	27.8%	43.0%	28.7%	2.5%
Deferred and other liabilities	0.5%	10.8%	0.1%	7.1%	1.1%
Total liabilities	38.2%	91.4%	64.0%	53.7%	17.5%
Preferred stock	3.0%	0.0%	0.0%	0.0%	0.0%
Adjusted equity (FIFO)	58.8%	8.6%	36.0%	46.3%	82.5%
Total liabilities and equities	100.0%	100.0%	100.0%	100.0%	100.0%

TABLE 3. Market Approach: Ratio Analysis (Adjusted)

	Company A	Company B	Company C	Company D	Subject Company
Sales ($000)	190,135	36,588	144,898	58,748	15,495
Leverage					
Assets to common equity	170.2%	1,159.0%	277.6%	216.1%	121.2%
Long-term liabilities to common equity	34.0%	485.6%	126.4%	77.4%	4.4%
EBIT to interest expectations	1.3	-0.3	1.6	1.7	N/A
Liquidity					
Current ratio	2.3	1.2	2.3	3.3	5.3
Quick ratio	1.3	0.3	1.1	1.5	4.3
Efficiency					
Sales to assets	2.5	2.4	1.6	1.5	1.3
Sales to employees ($000)	176.1	209.1	138.0	208.3	127.0
Receivable days	54.9	14.6	48.4	68.8	79.6
Inventory days	52.1	140.9	64.8	88.9	80.8
Payable days	48.7	23.4	28.0	40.4	70.8
Profitability					
Net profit margin	0.3%	-0.9%	0.9%	0.7%	2.8%
EBIT margin	2.4%	-0.4%	3.3%	2.8%	4.0%
Return on assets	0.7%	-2.2%	1.4%	1.1%	3.6%
Return on common equity	1.3%	-25.8%	3.9%	2.3%	4.4%

Notes:

N/A = Not Applicable/Available.

Total market capital equals long-term liabilities plus market capitalization of the equity.

TABLE 4. Market Approach: Historical DuPont Analysis (Adjusted)

	Company A	Company B	Company C	Company D	Subject Company
Net Profit Margin					
Prior three years	0.2%	-1.3%	-5.8%	6.8%	4.0%
Prior two years	0.2%	-1.2%	3.5%	5.4%	3.6%
Prior one year	-3.9%	1.7%	6.1%	2.1%	3.7%
Latest year	1.9%	0.2%	0.1%	2.8%	2.6%
12 months ended 1989	4.0%	-1.5%	1.1%	-2.3%	3.3%
Sales to Assets					
Prior three years	1.6	2.8	1.5	1.5	1.5
Prior two years	1.4	2.6	1.4	1.5	1.6
Prior one year	1.8	2.0	1.6	1.5	1.5
Latest year	1.8	2.2	1.5	1.6	1.4
12 months ended 1989	2.5	2.5	1.6	1.5	1.3
Return on Assets					
Prior three years	0.4%	-3.7%	-8.5%	9.9%	6.1%
Prior two years	0.3%	-3.1%	4.9%	8.0%	5.7%
Prior one year	-7.0%	3.6%	9.5%	3.2%	5.7%
Latest year	3.4%	0.5%	0.2%	4.6%	3.7%
12 months ended 1989	10.2%	-3.7%	1.7%	-3.4%	4.3%
Assets to Equity					
Prior three years	2.2	1.0	4.2	1.9	1.2
Prior two years	2.4	1.0	3.3	1.8	1.2
Prior one year	2.4	1.0	2.2	1.8	1.2
Latest year	2.2	1.0	2.7	1.8	1.2
12 months ended 1989	1.6	18.7	2.8	2.2	1.2
Return on Equity					
Prior three years	0.9%	-23.6%	-35.6%	18.9%	7.5%
Prior two years	0.7%	-63.4%	16.1%	14.6%	6.8%
Prior one year	-16.9%	66.3%	21.3%	5.8%	6.6%
Latest year	7.4%	11.3%	0.6%	8.3%	4.4%
12 months ended 1989	16.7%	-69.3%	4.9%	-7.3%	5.3%

Note:

For historical comparison purposes, income-statement and balance-sheet items have not been adjusted to reflect FIFO inventory accounting, capitalized operating leases, and nonrecurring items. As a result, the most recent-year performance will not match with prior exhibit.

TABLE 5. Market Approach: Historical-Growth Analysis (Adjusted)

Compound Annual Growth	Company A	Company B	Company C	Company D	Subject Company
Sales					
Latest quarter(s)	-3.4%	-1.1%	N/A	-5.8%	N/A
Latest year	-0.2%	1.0%	9.8%	8.2%	-4.9%
One year prior	2.1%	-6.3%	5.9%	7.4%	-2.6%
Two years prior	0.2%	-11.4%	0.1%	8.3%	-0.2%
Three years prior	-10.0%	-11.1%	-5.6%	13.6%	-0.5%
Total Asset					
Latest year	-1.0%	-8.5%	15.3%	-1.1%	2.4%
One year prior	-8.1%	0.2%	3.4%	2.4%	2.6%
Two years prior	-2.6%	-4.5%	0.0%	4.7%	2.4%
Three years prior	-7.0%	-8.0%	-6.2%	16.3%	1.8%
EBIT					
Latest year	-59.8%	-114.9%	117.1%	-56.8%	7.4%
One year prior	N/A	N/A	-41.2%	-31.7%	-20.9%
Two years prior	-5.5%	29.0%	-24.4%	- 35.0%	-16.2%
Three years prior	-1.0%	N/A	N/A	N/A	-10.5%

Note:
N/A = Not Applicable/Available.

Table 6. Market Approach: Market and EPS Data (Adjusted)

	Company A	Company B	Company C	Company D	Subject Company
Market	OTC	None	NYSE	OTC	N/A
Common shares outstanding (000's)	3,544	6,522	7,036	2,969	
Stock price as of new	$11.75	$0.50	$9.88	$6.25	
Total market capitalization	51,464	9,197	108,373	33,041	
Total market equity	41,638	3,261	69,480	18,557	
Annual C/S dividend	$0.00	$0.00	$0.22	$0.00	$221.00
C/S dividend yield	0.0%	0.0%	2.2%	0.0%	N/A
EPS Before Extraordinary Items					
FYE 5 years	($6.24)	$0.19	$0.26	$1.46	$50.69
FYE 4 years	($0.27)	($0.10)	($1.06)	$1.25	$215.43
FYE 3 years	($0.28)	($0.08)	$0.57	$0.69	$133.74
FYE 2 years	($2.20)	$0.10	$1.02	$0.39	$136.91
FYE 1 year	$0.49	$0.01	$0.03	$0.57	$119.48
12-month trailing 1989	$0.40	($0.07)	$0.22	($0.07)	$122.19

Notes:
N/A = Not Applicable/Available.
FYE = Fiscal year end.

TABLE 7. Market Approach: Market-Multiple Analysis (Adjusted)

Price/Market Multiples	Company A	Company B	Company C	Company D	Subject Company
Price to equity	0.9	2.5	2.1	1.0	N/A
Price to sales	0.22	0.09	0.48	0.32	N/A
Price to earnings	73.6	-9.5	55.2	43.7	N/A
Price to cash flow	8.7	7.8	9.4	6.5	N/A
Price to EBIT	9.1	-24.9	14.6	11.4	N/A
Price to EBDIT	4.8	5.2	6.4	4.6	N/A
Price to debt-free cash flow	6.3	4.7	7.2	5.4	N/A
Total Market Capital Multiples					
Total market capital to earnings	90.9	-26.9	86.1	77.8	N/A
Total market capital to cash flow	10.8	21.9	14.6	11.5	N/A
Total market capital to EBDIT	5.9	14.6	9.9	8.1	N/A
Total market capital to EBIT	11.3	-70.2	22.7	20.3	N/A
Total market capital to debt-free cash flow	7.7	13.3	11.2	9.6	N/A

Question and Answer Session

Question: How much time does it take to do a market valuation?

Wolf: A standard single-industry analysis takes about 100 hours of staff time and three to five days of a project manager's time—about 140 hours total. There are no short cuts. If you do not do a complete job, you will come up with a number that is not supportable. This could be very embarrassing if you wind up in litigation. I have some assignments that may take 500 to 1,000 hours.

Question: What is the best way to determine whether officers' compensation is reasonable?

Wolf: The experience of the person conducting the valuation is a key ingredient. I have seen enough numbers on officers' compensation that I have a pretty good feel for what is reasonable for a certain-size company. Beyond experience, there are several sources of information. The salaries of officers of publicly held comparable companies are published in their 10-K reports. In addition, the IRS has statistics on income.

Pratt: Another good source of information on compensation is a publication called *Growth Resources*. This is an annual study.

Question: Is there a close relation between greater risk and lower value?

Pratt: The higher the risk, the higher the required rate of return, and the higher the required rate of return, the lower the value for a given expected cash-flow stream. Whether that risk is linear, and the extent to which systematic or nonsystematic risk needs to be reflected, require subjective judgment. Of course, if you believe in the capital asset pricing model (CAPM), the relation is linear. But I submit to you that even if you believe the efficient markets hypothesis underlying the CAPM, when it comes to valuing closely held companies, the nonsystematic portion of the risk takes on significantly greater importance. You are not likely to get a thoroughly diversified portfolio of closely held companies so that you can diversify away all of the nonsystematic risk.

Question: What is the difference between valuing a service firm and valuing a product manufacturer?

Wolf: Because service firms and manufacturing firms are by nature so different, the valuation process must be adjusted to match the specific characteristics of the firm being valued. For example, service firms and manufacturing companies have different—but similar—multiples, but the factors that drive those multiples are different because of the nature of the products or services produced and the risks involved in those firms. For most service firms—such as insurance agencies, advertising agencies, and accounting firms—the customer base and employees are the key factors in the analysis. One must evaluate every aspect of the customer base. Are the customers repeat buyers? What is the profitability of that customer base? What is the growth in the number of customers? These factors will drive the multiples.

Question: Is debt a component of the valuation? Do you normally perform comparative analysis on a debt-free basis?

Wolf: Consideration of debt is a very important part of the valuation, especially in the era of LBOs. In the past couple of years, I have looked more at debt-free cash-flow multiples. There are a lot of private-market values being built into quality comparables, which are driven off a price-to-cash-flow or debt-free cash-flow basis; this may skew a minority multiple closer to a private-market or control value. It is prudent to look at the financing costs of the debt; the fair market value may be less than book value, and this could change the result.

Pratt: There are two cases in which one would use debt-free approaches to valuation. One is when you are doing a control valuation, and the control buyer of the company can change the capital structure. The other is in a minority valuation when the comparable companies have considerably different capital structures than the subject company.

Question: Please clarify the difference between enterprise comparables and minority comparables.

Wolf: Enterprise value is the value of a controlling interest. Therefore, the comparable value would be the value of a similar company with the control premium. The comparable for a minority interest is the value of shares of a similar company traded in the public market after adjusting for differences between the companies and the size of the transaction.

Discounted-Cash-Flow Approach to Valuation

Gregory A. Gilbert, CFA

According to finance texts, the fair market value of an ongoing business is the present worth of its expected cash flows. This simple conceptual framework is known as the discounted-cash-flow (DCF) valuation approach. The calculations necessary in a DCF approach are equally simple: Add the present values of the individual cash-flow estimates for each year from one to infinity. Although the DCF approach is the technically correct way to value a company, and although it is deceptively simple in theoretical execution, in practice it is quite complex and very subjective. In this presentation, I will discuss ways to try to overcome that subjectivity and make the valuation process more rational and objective.

The DCF Formula

The formula for the DCF approach is shown in equation (1) of **Exhibit 1**. The cash flow (CF) for each time period (n) is reduced to its present value using the compound-interest term $[(1+i)^n]$. The value of the company equals the sum of the present values for all periods, one to infinity. With a lot of work, it is usually possible to come up with an acceptable estimate of next year's cash flow. Each additional year becomes more difficult to estimate with an acceptable degree of accuracy.

In the real world it is very hard to work with time periods that extend to infinity and still maintain any semblance of rationality. Therefore, when the DCF method is used to value a business, the distant future is typically combined into one value representing the estimated sale price (terminal value) at some relatively close point in time. Thus, if equation (1) were to be ended at time period t instead of continuing to infinity, the formula would be modified as shown in equation (2). Typically, we estimate five or ten years of individual cash flows (CF$_1$, CF$_2$, CF$_3$, CF$_4$, . . . ,CF$_t$) and then estimate what the company could be sold for at the end of the period (TV$_t$). All of these estimates are then discounted to their present values at the valuation date, using standard compound-interest formulas, and the present values are added to-

gether to reach a valuation.

Having briefly reviewed the formulas behind the DCF approach, we will proceed to examine the individual components of the formulas and ways to estimate them.

Estimation of Cash Flows

The first step in the DCF process is the estimation of the individual cash flows. The definition of the cash-flow stream is critical to this type of analysis. Most people use *free cash flow* or *net cash flow*. These terms, which are used interchangeably, are normally defined as follows:

  projected adjusted income after income taxes;
  plus reported depreciation and amortization;
  less necessary capital expenditures;
  less necessary working capital increases; and
  less debt principal repayments, sometimes also adjusted for the issuance of new debt.

Stated in simplified form, *free cash flow* is the sum of the sources of cash, less the capital expenditures necessary to stay in business and continue to grow at the expected rate. These expenses must be included because a company cannot remain in business if its capital machinery gets old and outdated, nor can it grow without increases in working capital. The goal is to estimate recurring operating earnings and all cash-flow items associated with those earnings, including necessary capital expenditures. These estimates are the first area of subjectivity in the DCF valuation approach.

One way to estimate the annual cash flows is to use the company's financial history as the base for projections. There are many ways to use historical data. One of the best is to build a financial model of the company. The model may be very simple, for example a mathematical relation between sales and employees (either in dollar terms or unit terms), or it may be quite complex, incorporating non-linear relationships between the many variables. The process of estimating cash flows is similar to developing a five-year or ten-year business plan. It should address all key items in the income statement.

EXHIBIT 1. Equations

(1) *DCF Formula*

$$\text{Value} = \frac{CF_1}{(1+i)^1} + \frac{CF_2}{(1+i)^2} + \dots + \frac{CF_\infty}{(1+i)^\infty}$$

$$= \sum_{n=i}^{\infty} \frac{CF_n}{(1+i)^n}$$

Where:
- CF = cash flow
- i = discount rate
- n = time periods from one to infinity

(2) *Fair Market Value Estimate*

$$\text{Value} = \sum_{n=1}^{t} \frac{CF_n}{(1+i)^n} + \frac{TV_t}{(1+i)^t}$$

Where:
- CF = cash flow
- i = discount rate
- n = time periods, time = 1 to t
- TV = terminal value.

Source: Gregory A. Gilbert

In addition to estimation of net earnings, it should also involve an analysis of required capital equipment, cash to finance working capital, and any additional debt.

As well as making detailed estimates of the future, an appraiser must often make adjustments to accounting income to get the true economic income—that is, the cash flows generated by the operation of the business.

Perhaps the most common adjustment is to determine whether the *owner's compensation* is correct—in an economic sense. The appraiser must also look at the other employees and their compensation. Is the owner's grandmother really needed on the payroll? She might be very important if the product is Grandma's Cookies, and she is the only one who has the recipe. Otherwise, she might not be necessary to the company.

Contracts with related parties comprise the second area of adjustments. Leases are the most common type of contract in this category. Often, the business owner personally holds the land and building, and leases them to the business. There have been many attempts to make the lease rate close to a fair market value rate. In some instances, however, the lease rate is too high; in still other cases, too low. The arrangement often depends on the owner's personal tax situation. Appraisers have the responsibility to adjust the accounting income for differences between the actual lease rate and the economic lease rate. The

theory is that a new buyer could change the leases (or other types of contracts) to economic rates and more accurately calculate the income from the operation of the company.

The third type of adjustment is to remove from the income statement the income and expense related to *nonoperating assets*; for example, an airplane that is not used for business purposes but is owned and maintained by the company. The cost of maintaining and operating this asset must be removed from the income statement to avoid distortion of the appraiser's estimate of the company's operating income. Other types of assets might have income that must be removed from the income statement; still others may have both income and expense.

The fourth group of adjustments are those that must be made for *nonrecurring* income and expense. For example, if the firm incurred $200,000 in legal fees because of a lawsuit, and these costs are not likely to recur over the five- to ten-year time horizon, they should be eliminated.

The fifth type of adjustment an appraiser may have to make is for *capital deficiency* (or surplus). The appraiser must determine whether the firm's *operations* will need more (or less) capital and how the addition (or removal) of that capital would impact the income statement.

Finally, adjustments must often be made to *reconcile different accounting methods*. Not only are these adjustments part of the process of deriving the true economic income, or cash flow, figures, but they are also necessary to make the company's cash flow estimates conform with the data used to calculate the discount rate. Unfortunately, it is not always possible to reconcile different accounting methods when the companies are publicly owned. Thus, sometimes there is a conflict between these two reasons. In these cases, no adjustments should be made. The appraiser must make sure the company's cash flows conform as closely as possible to those of the publicly traded companies used in the derivation of the discount rate. In fact, an appraiser must sometimes construct two sets of estimated cash-flow statements: one adjusted statement that makes the closely held company look as much like a publicly traded company as possible, and another that attempts to show the economic reality.

Discount Rate

The second step in the DCF process is the determination of the discount rate.

Definition. A discount rate is defined as the rate of return an investor would require to be induced to invest in the cash-flow stream being discounted. There are six important aspects of discount rates. Discount rates

- are affected by the market;
- vary with time;
- depend on what is being discounted;
- must be risk adjusted;
- are based on yields available on alternative investments; and
- are inflation adjusted.

External factors. Three basic external factors affect discount rates: (1) general economic conditions; (2) yields available on alternative investments; and (3) industry conditions and outlook. The process of analyzing the external factors provides the appraiser with a sense of what might affect the discount rate. The answers to a few basic questions may provide a wealth of information. For example, is the industry going to grow at 5 percent? At 10 percent? Is it stable? Is it shrinking? How will the industry's growth affect the expectations for cash flow? If management says that the subject company is going to grow at 10 percent a year for the next 10 years, but the industry is stable or declining, that projection may not make sense.

Internal factors. There are three internal factors that affect discount rates: (1) financial risk, (2) operating risk, and (3) the risk associated with the estimation of the cash-flow stream.

1. *Financial risk* has five basic inputs: leverage, coverage, turnover, return, and liquidity. The adjustments to the discount rate are fairly obvious; higher risk in the financial measures must lead to higher discount rates.

2. *Operating risk* has the following basic inputs: management, accounting methods, stability of markets, customer base, and competitive position. The appraiser must incorporate into the discount rate his assessment of the capability of management, whether the accounting methods are conservative or aggressive, and so forth. For example, if aggressive accounting treatments that increase risk are left in the cash-flow projections, a higher discount rate should be used. On the other hand, a very stable customer base might lead one to reduce the discount rate. Similarly, if there is a lot of competition, the rate should be higher; if there is very little competition, the rate should be lower.

3. *Risk associated with the estimation of the cash-flow stream.* If there is considerable uncertainty surrounding the 10-year sales and

earnings forecast, as would be true with a start-up company, the discount rate must be higher to account for this risk. On the other hand, if the company has a stable operating history and established relationships, the greater certainty of the forecast should be reflected in a lower discount rate.

Components. The discount rate is a function of three components: (1) a risk-free rate, (2) a general risk premium covering both equity risk and industry risk, and (3) a factor for company-specific risk.

1. The *risk-free rate* is the easiest factor to identify objectively. It is generally recognized that there are three measures of the risk-free rate: long-term government bonds, intermediate-term Treasury notes, and short-term Treasury bills. The appropriate risk-free instrument to use in the construction of a discount rate is the one that matches the investment horizon. For an equity investment with a long time horizon, a 30-year bond might be appropriate. Often a typical financial horizon is five to seven years; in that case, intermediate-term notes would be appropriate. Finally, if an appraiser is valuing something like a patent that only has a few years left before expiration, short-term Treasury bills might be the appropriate measure of the risk-free rate. The analyst must determine what makes sense.

2. It is harder for the appraiser to identify the appropriate *general risk premium*. There are four basic methods that appraisers use to estimate this premium.
   - One of the four commonly used methods is *direct comparison*. This method involves developing a discount rate from actual transactions. Unfortunately, it is often hard to find the necessary data.
   - The second of the four methods is the *inverse of a price/cash-flow ratio plus growth*. This method involves five steps. The first step is to find a list of publicly traded companies that are enough like the company being appraised to be considered similar or comparative, or if you are really lucky, comparable. The second step is to calculate price/cash-flow ratios for the similar publicly traded companies. The third step is to invert the price/cash-flow ratio to get a cash-flow/price ratio. A cash-flow/price

ratio is really a capitalization rate. (Note that price = cash-flow/cap rate, or cap rate = cash-flow/price.) The difference between a capitalization rate and a discount rate is growth. The relationship is: cap rate plus growth equals discount rate. The fourth step is to estimate the growth rate from the similar publicly traded companies. Note that the growth rate referenced here is the expected (not observed), long-term growth rate. The final step in the derivation of the discount rate is to add the growth rate to the cash-flow/price ratio.

- The third approach to developing a general risk premium is to use *historical stock market return data*. The Ibbotson-Sinquefield studies are the normal source of historical returns.[1] The differential between returns on stocks and a risk-free rate is believed to be a measure of the extra reward accruing to investors for assuming equity risk. For appraisal purposes the general equity risk premium is normally estimated as the difference between the arithmetic mean return for small-capitalization stocks and the same return for government bonds.

- The fourth method for estimating the general risk-premium portion of a discount rate is the *capital asset pricing model* (CAPM). This is perhaps the most common method used by appraisers. The formula for the CAPM is as follows:

$$R_e = R_f + (R_m - R_f)B$$

where:

R_e = expected return,

R_f = expected risk-free rate,

R_m = expected return on the market, and

B = expected systematic risk (commonly called beta).

The needed inputs to CAPM are obtained from several sources. The return on the market (R_m) is usually derived from historical stock market returns (Ibbotson and Sinquefield 1989). Betas are only published for publicly traded companies, so a beta

applicable to an individual company must be estimated, usually using the betas of similar publicly traded companies. The selection of beta is critical to the accurate calculation of a discount rate, yet the appraiser has little to guide the selection process. Further, CAPM theory is based on estimates of expected returns (R_f and R_m) and expected betas. In actual practice we can only use historical returns and historical betas. Unfortunately, both returns and betas vary over time, which casts suspicion on using historical measures.

In the theoretical framework of the CAPM, the specific return (alpha) is assumed to be diversified away for efficient portfolios. It is probably still relevant for individual stocks, however.

I remain skeptical about using the CAPM to derive the discount rate because the key inputs are so subjective. The reason for using a model like the CAPM to estimate the discount rate is to increase the *objectivity* of the process. Ironically, the subjective decisions necessary in the CAPM process may increase the *subjectivity* of the final discount rate instead of the objectivity.

3. The hardest part of the determination of a discount rate is to estimate the *company-specific risk premium*. Unfortunately, there are no objective data to help reach an appropriate company-specific risk premium (or alpha, in CAPM parlance). Experience is very valuable. Each company's situation must be evaluated separately, and all risk factors must be recognized and incorporated into the company-specific premium. Just as the stock market determines a different beta for each publicly traded company, the appraiser must determine a different beta (or industry beta plus individual alpha) for each subject company.

Terminal Value

Once the periodic cash flows have been estimated and the discount rate has been chosen, the first term in equation (2) of Exhibit 1 can be calculated. The last piece of information needed to complete the discounted-cash-flow calculation is the terminal value.

[1]See Ibbotson and Sinquefield (1989); data is updated annually by Ibbotson Assoicates.

As stated earlier, the terminal value is the value of the company in year t as if it were to be sold in year t. There are several ways to estimate terminal value.

The most common method is to "capitalize" the cash flow expected in the next period (period "t + 1"). In equation (1), if the growth rate of the cash-flow stream is constant over time periods one to infinity, and if the growth is small relative to the discount rate, equation (1) simplifies to:

$$\text{Value} = \frac{CF_1}{i - g}$$

Where:

CF_1 = cash flow in period 1(the next period);
i = discount rate; and
g = constant growth rate from time $t = 1$ to time $t = $ infinity.

This formula is essentially the Gordon-Shapiro Model. In business appraisal, it is generally shown as follows:

$$\text{Terminal Value} = \frac{\text{Cash Flow}_{t-1}}{\text{Capitalization Rate}}$$

Where:

Capitalization Rate = Discount Rate – Growth.

The cash flow used in the formula is the *next year's* cash flow. The capitalization rate is risk adjusted and growth adjusted. The formula is that for single-period capitalization. The cash flow is assumed to last forever, as is the growth. The terminal value given by the formula is as of the date in the future and must be discounted to the present. Specifically, the capitalized terminal value is as of the end of year t (not "t + 1," even though the cash flow must be for year "t + 1") and must be discounted to the present value as of the appraisal date.

The capitalization rate is a very important variable. In a DCF approach it is not uncommon to see 50 to 80 percent of the calculated value come from the residual value term. Care is also important because with capitalization rates normally somewhere in the 10 to 30 percent range, a small change in the capitalization rate will have a big impact on value.

Capitalization rates, like discount rates, are determined by the market, vary with time, depend on what is being capitalized, and have a very long time-horizon expected growth rate. The normal selection of a capitalization rate at this point in the DCF approach is to take the discount rate developed earlier and subtract an estimate of long-term growth. The long-term nature of the growth rate cannot be over-emphasized. If long-term inflation expectations are 4 to 5 percent, the growth rate will be a minimum of 4 to 5 percent—that is, no *real* growth. If there is real growth on top of that, the analyst must decide how long the company can grow at a rate greater than the population growth rate, which is only 1 to 2 percent, and what the extra increase would average if viewed over a 50-year time horizon. IBM and McDonald's have both grown for a long time at a rate higher than population growth plus inflation, but they are very unusual companies. Most companies cannot do that.

As an alternative to the capitalization process for estimation of terminal value, one may assume that the company will be worth its book value at the end of time t. If a company is ever going to be worth book value, time t is probably as good a time as any; at least it is several years away. (Nonetheless, it will be worthwhile to check the expected return on equity in time period t to see if book value is a reasonable estimate of value. Do not use a book value as a terminal value if you are expecting a return on equity 10 years from now that is double today's industry rate of return.) The future book value must be discounted back to its present value as of the valuation date.

Another method for calculating terminal value is to use an industry rule of thumb. If you use a rule of thumb, be sure it makes sense, or at least does not offend common sense.

Conclusion

The DCF valuation approach is theoretically the most "correct" valuation approach. It is necessary for the appraiser to use great care in the estimation of cash flows, discount rates, and terminal values. The expected cash flows must be rigorously developed and supported with all available data.

The CAPM may help the appraiser, but it must be applied with wisdom and the benefit of experience in recognizing and quantifying investment risk. Company-specific risk must not be forgotten. Likewise, other methods may be used to help develop discount rates, or to corroborate rates reached through use of the CAPM.

The estimation of terminal value is perhaps the most crucial part of the DCF approach, because normally over half of the ultimate appraised value comes from the terminal value. The capitalization rate and its growth component are critical in the development of an accurate terminal value.

Question and Answer Session

Question: What range of discount rates should be used in a DCF analysis?

Gilbert: The answer depends on the company. When you are dealing with start-up companies, you look to rates expected by venture capitalists—perhaps rates as high as 100 percent per year, or even more. The fact that these are very high rates implies—among other things—that you do not have a lot of faith in the cash-flow stream being discounted. For companies that are not start-ups, the rate normally falls in the 10- to 30-percent range.

Question: Should the discount rate be pre-tax or post-tax?

Gilbert: The answer depends on whether the cash flows are net of taxes. Most appraisers use free cash-flow and post-tax discount rates.

Question: Is it appropriate to use a higher discount rate for the terminal value to account for a higher risk so far into the future?

Gilbert: It makes a lot of sense conceptually to use a higher discount rate, but you almost never see it done.

Pratt: This is a controversial area; there is no right answer to this question. One approach to DCF analysis is to use a different discount rate for each year of cash flow, recognizing the increasing risk as the estimates are further into the future. This approach implies a different and generally higher rate for the terminal value. Some people advocate using a constant rate across all years. No matter which approach you adopt, the rate must relate to your assessment of the risk of each cash flow. To the extent that you judge the terminal value to be of higher risk, then you might consider using a higher discount rate.

Question: Is the value derived in the DCF analysis a minority-interest value or a controlling-interest value?

Pratt: Theoretically, if you use the CAPM, you are going to end up with a publicly traded minority-interest value before adjusting for lack of marketability

and for control.[2] You have to determine how much of the difference in value between control and minority interests is because of higher expected cash flows under the new owner, and how much of it is because of a lower discount rate that results from your having control. The consensus seems to be that most of the difference comes from higher expected cash flows, but there is also some difference in the discount rate. A control owner might use a discount rate that is 100 to 200 basis points lower.

Gilbert: The value depends on whether you use a control discount rate or a minority-interest discount rate. For example, if you adjust for owner's compensation and add back a huge increment because the owner is taking excessive compensation, then you have probably captured a good portion of the control premium in the cash-flow stream (numerator). Similarly, if you are valuing a minority interest and you do not adjust for excessive owner's compensation (on the theory that the minority owners do not have the right to require the controlling person to take a lower salary), a lot of the minority-interest discount is in the numerator.

Question: If, instead of using net free cash flow as the numerator in your cash-flow projection you use operating cash flow or net income, what is the proper discount rate?

Gilbert: Normally, I simply add 5 percentage points. It is an entirely empirical approach; there is no theoretical basis for 5 points, it just seems to work out right most of the time.

Question: What is wrong with the CAPM?

Gilbert: I would start with the efficient markets theory. I do not believe the efficient markets theory holds in either its strong form or semi-strong form. I also have problems with other underlying CAPM assumptions. I do not like the fact that we have to use historical data when the theory requires expectational data. Nor do I like the assumption that anyone may borrow at the risk-free rate; that is not a realistic assumption. Further, I am not convinced that it is valid to use CAPM on a portfolio of just common stocks. After all, the theory was developed for portfolios made up of every asset, not just financial

---

[2]See Dr. Pratt's presentation, pp. 38-52.

assets that are easily measured. To then use CAPM on a single company presses the theory one step further.

Then, there are problems with betas. First, they are not stationary. Second, I am not sure that we are measuring beta correctly. Is price volatility the right measure of risk? Maybe earnings volatility or dividend volatility would be better. The list of problems goes on.

Question: Is the arbitrage pricing theory (APT) any better?

Gilbert: I think you wind up with similar problems using APT as you do with the CAPM.

Pratt: The APT is not widely used in the valuation of closely held businesses, but it is an extension of the CAPM. The consensus is that the APT is not far enough developed to be of practical use, but I would not rule it out; it is something everyone should be aware of because it is going to be developed more in the future.

Question: Would you still use 20- or 30-year government bonds for the risk-free rate on a long-term horizon if the yield curve is inverted?

Gilbert: Yes—although I do not like to deal with an inverted yield curve in valuing a long-term equity.

Pratt: You have a much bigger problem with an inverted yield curve if you are using the 30-day Treasury-bill rate because it is not a stable rate. Therefore, the more inverted the yield curve, the more it augers toward using a long-term as opposed to a short-term rate as your base rate.

Question: You stated that the DCF valuation approach is very subjective. Isn't the market approach, with the judgment required in selecting comparables and adjusting their statements, also subjective? Given the level of subjectivity in so many areas of DCF analysis—that is, revenue and margin projections, discount rates, estimation of terminal value, and so forth—can DCF analysis be accurate enough to be used as anything more than a smell test for other valuation measures?

Gilbert: Subjectivity is important. Without subjectivity, my computer would do everything, and everyone in this room would be out of a job. There is a lot of subjectivity in every appraisal approach. The market approach has a lot of subjectivity when it comes to picking the correct multiple. A good set of data will narrow the choices to a reasonable set, but that last step—from the narrowed range to "the" number—depends on subjectivity.

Question: Is it appropriate to make adjustments to income for a minority valuation?

Gilbert: If you make adjustments, some of the control premium may be contained in the adjustments. So if you are doing a minority appraisal, you have to consider a minority discount. If you do not make the adjustments to income for a minority valuation, most of the minority discount will probably be captured in the cash flows; therefore, you do not need to make as large a minority discount.

Question: Are necessary capital expenditures a part of the numerator in the standard DCF equation? If so, do you use Generally Accepted Accounting Principles (GAAP) capital expenditures or economic capital expenditures? For example, how do you recommend treating capital expenditures financed by operating leases such as aircraft or a truck fleet?

Gilbert: Assuming the leases are good, fair-market-value, third-party leases, they should already be included in the cash-flow stream. I prefer to use economic capital expenditures rather than GAAP because GAAP accounting is not very relevant in appraisal terms.

Pratt: The answer to that part of the question is unequivocal. In financial analysis, we are trying to deal with the economic realities of the situation; accounting data are simply a starting point. We have to determine our best estimate of economic reality. In theory, you would treat operating leases as part of capital expenditures. But to do that, you have to subtract all of the payments on the operating leases from the income stream. Unless they are a very significant item, they are going to be recognized in the income stream anyway. So although you would make that adjustment theoretically, as a practical matter, more often than not, that adjustment is not made.

Question: If optimistic cash flows are used, should the discount rate be higher than the rate used for more conservative cash flows?

Gilbert: Yes. Absolutely.

Question: Do you use probability trees as an alternative to adjusting your discount rate to reflect errors in estimation?

Gilbert: It depends on the audience: Never use a probability tree on a judge. On the other hand, if you have a very sophisticated corporate CFO who might understand a probability tree, use it.

Question: What is the best way to value a contingent liability?

Gilbert: The best way to handle a contingent liability, like a lawsuit that will bankrupt the company, is to value the company before the contingent liability and then adjust that for the value of the contingent liability. A probability tree is superb for this kind of thing. Of course, the biggest problem is assigning the probabilities.

Adjusted-Book-Value Approach to Valuation

David W. Nicholas

The adjusted-book-value approach should be distinguished from other approaches that rely on the balance sheet. For example, a method relying on book value, which is nothing more than an accumulation of historical earnings that were not otherwise disposed of, does not reflect fair market value, except by coincidence. It should also be distinguished from the price-to-book method, which is an approach to value that relies on the market as opposed to the summation of the asset values. The adjusted-book-value approach should also be differentiated from any sort of liquidation valuation, which typically represents the value that would pertain if the assets were to be separated from the business and sold in the open market. The value of assets in the open market does not accord the assets the full consideration they warrant in terms of their contributive worth to the continuing business.

The adjusted-balance-sheet approach to valuation involves a determination of the going-concern fair market value of all the assets and liabilities of a business. Typically, not as much attention is applied to intangible assets and liabilities as perhaps should be, but in theory, at least, all the assets and liabilities of the firm need to be addressed. In the valuation of closely held businesses, the adjusted-balance-sheet approach is not always relevant. But it is used, and one should know about it. The adjusted-balance-sheet method values the intrinsic, or contributive, worth of the assets. The valuation should include both the stated and contingent assets and liabilities. The difference between the assets and the liabilities is the adjusted net worth of the business, incorporating current values as opposed to those set forth by the historical-cost accounting model.

Anyone who relies substantially on the historical-cost balance sheet in the valuation process is doomed to failure—and perhaps embarrassment. One of the deficiencies of the historical-cost balance sheet is that it is unlikely to reflect intangible assets. The adjusted-book-value approach is appropriate when one is concerned with the full value of the business enterprise or a controlling interest in the enterprise. On occasion, it may be appropriate to use this methodology in the valuation of a minority interest—if you have the time and resources. Such application, however, is infrequent—if it exists at all. This approach is most appropriate for the valuation of a holding company—particularly one in which the current returns available to shareholders do not adequately reflect the fair market value of the business in its entirety. It is appropriate to pierce the corporate veil and look at the underlying assets of the firm to determine what investment might be justified over the longer term.

The Assets

The first step in the adjusted-book-value approach is to value the various asset classes. I will summarize the major considerations in valuing each asset category.

Cash. As a general rule, cash is treated as cash. It is gratifying to have something simple in the process. In all other valuation approaches, cash is an additive factor to the extent that there is excess accumulated cash; it is something that must be brought into play after the valuation of the operating business has been accomplished. In this approach, all of the current assets, regardless of their excess or deficiency, are reflected in the summation.

Accounts receivable. Generally, accounts receivable are considered at their face value. Of course, this presumes that conscientious attention is accorded the collection of accounts receivable in the ordinary course of business. It is appropriate, from time to time, to check whether the accounts receivable are in fact collectible and to make a judgment regarding the timing of those collections. This is a particular problem when a firm is near bankruptcy. When a firm announces it is about to declare bankruptcy, or if it appears obvious to those doing business with the firm that it may be headed in that direction, accounts receivable become very difficult to collect. In fact, if there is financial distress in the situation, it would be wise to look skeptically at inventories and all other current asset accounts as well.

Inventories. This is a very troublesome area. The valuation of inventories involves complex issues that make this asset class extraordinarily difficult to treat on a time- and cost-efficient basis. The best I can do in the time available today is provide the sources of information on how to conduct the valuation. The controlling document from the tax side, Revenue Procedure 77-12, stipulates the treatment that should be accorded manufacturing inventories; it also covers retail inventories, which constitute a significantly different kind of valuation problem.

There are several steps required in valuing manufacturing inventories. First, raw materials are valued at their most recent cost (if that cost could indeed be realized). If the inventory is like a commodity, it may be reintroduced into the market, and the cost of purchasing the inventory may be recouped. Second, work-in-process inventory gets special treatment. It may be approached either from its cost (plus an allowance for the value that has been embedded by the manufacturer) or from its ultimate sale price. Third, finished-goods inventory typically is appraised by determining the amount that will be received from its sale in the ordinary course of business, less any normal discounts and allowances; less the cost the new owner incurs in holding, transporting, and effecting the sale of the inventoried products; and less an amount representing a return on the investment in the inventory during the holding and disposal period. The latter deduction is debatable because that return may already be incorporated in the selling price of the goods. Finally, the buyer's share of the anticipated profit should be deducted.

Included in the determined value should be only that portion of the ultimate profit to be realized by the seller prior to the imagined transaction. The AICPA has issued a document on the valuation of inventory, *Accounting Research Bulletin* (Number 43, Chapter 4), which is essentially the same as Revenue Procedure 77-12. Because it is not always practical to spend the time and money necessary to appraise the inventory in detail, there are alternatives. For example, if the firm is on a FIFO basis (i.e., first in, first out), one may use book value as a surrogate for fair market value, assuming the inventory turns over rather quickly. Correspondingly, if the firm is on an LIFO basis (i.e., last in, first out), one may simply reinstate the LIFO reserve to approximate FIFO-based inventory to arrive at a reasonable substitute for fair market value.

Other current assets. Normally, these assets are valued at their book value. This would be true for deposits and accruals that benefit the firm for some reasonable period of time in the future. Certain assets in this category, however, should be carefully scrutinized—for example, notes from shareholders in a small, closely held company. Often, there is no intention of ever repaying them. One should be very careful about incorporating these as legitimate assets of the firm. This is particularly relevant when valuing a minority position—recognizing, of course, that the minority investor has no claim on the assets and cannot influence their existence or realization.

Fixed tangible assets. Property-, plant-, and equipment-value estimates are an important part of the adjusted-book-value approach to valuing a closely held business. I will outline the basic procedures.

Land is valued as if it were vacant and available for development to its highest and best use. This is done by looking in the market for evidence of transactions involving similar pieces of land. With enough information, one may approximate value by using the value per square foot or per acre observed in the marketplace. One frequent problem is that the property being appraised has not been developed to its highest and best use—on the contrary, the improvements detract from the value of the land. There are several ways of dealing with this issue. One simple approach is to use assessed values; that is, the determination of fair market value for property-tax purposes before application of an equalization ratio. I would avail myself of that information whenever possible.

Buildings and other civic improvements—basically site and land improvements—are usually valued on the basis of replacement costs less the various elements of depreciation, deterioration, and obsolescence that may be evident. In the cost approach to value, start with an amount that is intended to reflect the cost of a new, equivalent asset and then systematically reduce that cost to reflect the fact that the asset is not new, that it may suffer in terms of its age and condition or its utility to the business, or that it may be incapable of generating an adequate return on its investment.

There is a difference between replacement cost and reproduction cost. Reproduction indicates duplication precisely in kind—i.e., replication. Replacement involves substituting utility, which may require a considerably different facility. For instance, the reproduction cost of a five-story mill building with 36-inch rubble stone foundations would be the cost of constructing that very building, although you probably could not find anybody to build it for you today even if you wanted to. The replacement cost of that building would be the cost of a single-story, tilt-up concrete kind of facility optimally suited to the manufacturing process.

Open-market transactions of improved real estate—that is, manufacturing plants—are not usually very helpful in this type of valuation because they essentially represent liquidations. The buildings are usually empty or will be empty; and they are purchased by an array of buyers with differing motivations, expectations, and potential with regard to the utilization of the property. Open-market transactions are essentially liquidating values, whereas what we are looking for in a going-concern appraisal is the contributive worth of the building, presuming the occupant is using it optimally.

A recent insurance appraisal of the structure is often helpful because *actual cash value* is equal to replacement value less depreciation (usually only physical depreciation). Therefore, an insurance appraisal will lead to a ballpark number for the plant. As in the case of land values, assessed values may be used as an approximation if one is reasonably confident that the person making the assessment is competent and conscientious.

The cost approach is typically used to value machinery and equipment in a continued-use or going-concern valuation of plant, property, and equipment. An alternative to the cost approach to valuing an asset is to find out what price similar assets are trading for in the market and then add to that amount the cost of installing the asset and getting it running in your location with the balance of the assets. Developing this approach obviously requires both time and contacts.

Nonoperating assets. Nonoperating assets are defined as assets that are extraneous to the operating requirements of the business. The business would operate just as efficiently—in fact, it might be more efficient—if it did not hold these assets. They are treated separately in all approaches to value. Long-term investment securities are an example of assets in this category. These assets may be sizable. For example, I recently encountered a small specialty advertising firm that had a book net worth of $3.5 million, of which long-term investment securities represented $0.75 million. A quick look at the nature of those securities, however, suggested that their fair market value might have been around $2.5 million.

Another commonly encountered nonoperating asset is excess land—land that may have been acquired with the expectation of expansion or development but is not being used. Its fair market value should be determined separately from the operating assets of the business. A common example of a nonoperating asset is a condominium in, say, Vail, Colorado. If it is on the balance sheet at all, it is invariably listed as the corporate education center; the chairman and the president go out there to "educate" themselves on the slopes periodically. Lear jets and the like are often hidden in the transportation equipment account—they must get used to go to Vail. These assets must be treated separately.

There are different opinions about what to do with these assets, depending on whether you are doing a majority or a minority valuation. Certainly, for a controlling-interest valuation, assuming an exchange-of-ownership situation, a new owner would be able to do wonderful things with these assets, so they must be included in the valuation. On the other hand, you might not accord them any more than their book value, or perhaps a discounted fair market value in a minority-interest valuation because the minority shareholder has no ability to influence or access those assets. If there were an announced plan to dispose of such assets, there would ultimately be additional cash in the business. Then, arguably, you might want to include the fair market value. Certainly, in the other valuation approaches, the income effects of the ownership of these assets, as well as the balance-sheet effects, must be treated.

Intangible assets. One should identify and appraise as many of the intangible assets of the business as possible. They should be valued discretely with whatever approach is appropriate. Generally, the market approach is not very helpful in dealing with intangible assets because they cannot be readily disassociated from the business and separately sold. Therefore, an income or a cost approach must be used. All of this leaves the appraiser with the problem of goodwill. One cannot get at the value of "softer" intangible assets without determining the total economic value of the business. This can be accomplished through the excess-earnings approach embodied in Revenue Ruling 68-609. The excess-earnings approach to valuing goodwill is illustrated in **Table 1**. Unfortunately, this type of approach is circular. If the overall return reflected in the relation between earnings and the aggregate value of the business is a certain percentage of the weighted average returns on it, various asset components must be the same number. Otherwise, the model makes no economic sense. This is not a very satisfying approach, but it is one alternative.

The Liabilities

The liabilities must be valued with the same care as the assets. I will describe the major considerations involved in treating long-term liabilities.

Valuing long-term debt is fairly straightforward using the classic bond discount model. This is simply a matter of discounting the principal and interest requirements of debt service to present worth at an appropriate market rate. Of course, the current portion of long-term debt should be included. In a controlling-interest valuation, the discount or premium

TABLE 1. The Excess Earnings Approach to the Value of Goodwill			
Near-term debt-free net income after taxes			$100
Less required returns on tangible and identifiable intangible assets			
Net working capital	$200 x 0.07 =	$14	
Fixed tangible assets	$500 x 0.09 =	45	
Identifiable intangible assets	$200 x 0.12 =	24	83
"Excess" earnings available as a return on goodwill			$ 17
Capitalized to value at an appropriate rate			
	$17 ÷ 0.17 =		$100

Note:

Total net asset value (invested capital) is equal to $1,000. Given this amount and income of $100, the weighted-average return on investment is 10 percent, the capitalization rate yielding the value of the business enterprise.

Source: Revenue Ruling 68-609, 26 CFR, 1.1001-1. (See also A.R.M. 34, superseded.)

associated with that particular liability must be incorporated in the valuation. In a minority-interest case, the traditional approach is to ignore any advantage that might be viewed as favorable financing. In my opinion, minority shareholders benefit when the firm pays less interest than it might have to pay if it issued the debt in the current public market; they benefit because the firm is able to retain the saved interest and, perhaps, enhance dividends. Whatever the situation, the contra-liability or asset must be dealt with in some fashion. Clearly, if the interest rate being paid exceeds the market rate, the increased cost must be deducted to more adequately reflect the true worth of the company.

Deferred taxes. The valuation of these liabilities depends upon the situation of the firm. If you choose not to treat deferred taxes as a true liability or obligation of the firm—for example, if the firm is in a growing mode and may never actually pay those taxes—there is a concomitant enhancement of stockholder's equity by simply eliminating it as a liability. On the other hand, if you are convinced that the future of the firm would call for the payment of

the amounts deferred, these liabilities should be included in the valuation, either on a book-value basis or on a projected basis. Frankly, the latter would be an extraordinarily difficult task.

Contingent assets and liabilities. The valuation of contingent claims is a matter of determining the amount, timing, and probability of occurrence of the claim, and then discounting the cash flows back to their present worth. This is very difficult to do because virtually no one tells you the truth, even if they know it. As a result, contingent liabilities and assets often are simply not included in valuations.

Determining Value

Once the values of the assets and liabilities have been determined, calculating the controlling-interest value is simple. The full control value of the business enterprise is the difference between the assets and the liabilities. No control premium is necessary because the full contributive value of each of the assets has been captured, and the true liabilities of the firm have been addressed in economic terms. Even in a full business enterprise valuation, it might be appropriate to apply a marketability discount. This is because even though it is easier to sell entire businesses than it is to sell parts of businesses, it is not always easy to identify and inform buyers for an entire business on a timely basis. Sometimes it proves to be quite difficult to sell a closely held business. So, arguably, a discount for lack of marketability might be appropriate. Certainly, in the appraisal of majority interests that have diminished control—or perhaps lack true control—a marketability discount is appropriate.

The same subtractive process applies to the calculation of the value of minority interests, but the difference must be adjusted not only for marketability concerns, but also to account for the minority position. Minority investments take fairly deep discounts because it is very difficult to sell a minority position in a closely held business. After all, who wants to go into business with four brothers who inherited the business from their father? A proportional share of the full value of the business enterprise must be adjusted downward to account for the fact that a minority-interest valuation should reflect what an investor would pay if, in fact, the stock were available and freely traded in the open market. Dr. Pratt discusses premia and discounts in his presentation.[1]

[1]See Dr. Pratt's presentation, pages 38-52.

Conclusion

The adjusted-book-value approach to valuation is a useful means of estimating the fair market value of a business enterprise in certain circumstances, particularly for holding companies and when the charge is to appraise the full value of the enterprise or a control position therein. It can be a time-consuming technique, and one calling for several types and levels of expertise not typically resident in the business valuer's bag of tricks. Sadly, it is often misapplied; as a result, it yields results that should not be accorded the weight that can attach to well-reasoned market or income approaches to value.

Question and Answer Session

Question: How can assets or estimated asset values far in excess of current market values be justified when the business does not have a history of earnings on those assets? That is, aren't the assets only as good as the income generated on them?

Nicholas: The adjusted-balance-sheet approach, which involves the valuation of the individual assets on a discrete basis, cannot stand on its own. One must test the viability of the appraiser's conclusion. Asset values are very much contingent upon the earnings of the firm and the expectancy of the continuity of reasonable returns on investment.

Question: In what situation would liquidation value be the fair market value?

Nicholas: If you have a situation in which the firm is not currently capable of providing an appropriate return on investment, you have some sense of what the value of the net assets may be, and you satisfy yourself that future earnings are not going to provide an appropriate return on that level of investment, you then must consider the possibility that the firm obtains its greatest value in liquidation. It is a judgment call as to when that occurs. Most appraisers will make rough estimates of the net proceeds of liquidation, and what may become fair market value when the earnings are not there. I have not encountered that situation often. What occur more frequently are situations in which the earnings are deficient in some way, and the asset value conclusions must be adjusted downward so that their value, still greater than liquidation value, is accommodated in the context of the total economic worth of the business.

Pratt: Generally in minority-interest valuations the courts have accorded very little weight to the value of excess assets. That was certainly the situation of the *U.S. News & World Report* case, where the appraisers accorded little weight to the excess assets and the court upheld that treatment because the minority stockholders simply cannot force a redeployment of those excess assets.[2]

[2]Charles S. Foltz, et. al. v. U.S. News & World Report, Inc., et. al., and David B. Richardson, et. al., v. U.S. News & World Report, Inc., et. al., U.S. District Court, District of Columbia, Civil Actions No. 84-0447 and 85-2195, June 22, 1987. (The *Foltz* case, a class action, dealt with the years 1973 through 1980; the *Richardson* case, not a class action, covered 1981.)

Question: If assets are adjusted upward, what should one do about the contingent tax liability?

Nicholas: As a general rule, if the valuation is for an ongoing business, the contingent tax liability is not considered. The fair market value of an asset is determined on a pre-tax basis. For example, a machine is not valued at cost new, less depreciation, less taxes. Nor is land valued that way. On the other hand, if there is a reasonable expectation that the assets will be disposed of, the tax effects should be considered. If the firm intends to dispose of a group of assets in the near future, I would determine their fair market value allowing for tax effects, and the result would be a net-realizable or exit value.

Question: Adjustments to the liability side of the balance sheet are often overlooked. How should one treat an industrial revenue bond (IRB) debt that carries a low tax-advantaged rate, yet trades at par? Similarly, how should one treat lower-than-market-rate Employee Stock Ownership Plan (ESOP) debt because of the tax advantages that the ESOP may get in its borrowing rates?

Nicholas: Both of these situations should be treated carefully. Often those same low IRB rates are available to anyone in the marketplace—that is, anyone who would be willing to come in and set up a facility and give employment to 1,000 people. Although the interest rate may seem extraordinarily low relative to other forms of debt, its true market value may be consistent with its stated rate. An adjustment should be made if the interest rate is no longer available. For example, some firms took out ESOP loans before the law changed, and they would not otherwise qualify for the favorable rate today. One should make an adjustment for that fact. The adjustment would be a contra-liability (or asset) equal to the present value of the differential in interest payments.

Question: Are the excess assets in a pension plan an asset of the corporation?

Nicholas: That takes a legal answer. In many of the LBOs I have been involved in, there has been substantial consideration accorded excess assets in pension funds. If it is possible to retire a plan, substitute an appropriate plan for the employees covered, and extract those funds—and there is no legal constraint—then of course they should be included as an asset in the valuation.

Question: What valuation method is most acceptable to the courts and the IRS? Is the adjusted-balance-sheet approach acceptable to the IRS for estate- and gift-tax valuations?

Nicholas: My general sense is that the courts prefer to see a well-executed market approach. They are only recently beginning to understand and accept the discounted-cash-flow (DCF) approach, which is the income alternative. They are not likely to be very excited about an adjusted-book-value approach, unless it is for a real estate holding company or something of that sort. The IRS is accustomed to seeing what is, in essence, an adjusted-book-value approach, because buyers are permitted to adjust the basis of the assets acquired in many forms of transaction. The taxpayer has to perform an allocation of his purchase price, so one goes through this routine. I think it would be very extraordinary for them to accept this kind of approach for estate- and gift-tax valuations.

Pratt: On the other hand, at the field level, the IRS will accept any approach that results in the highest value. In the *Watts* case, in which I testified in Atlanta, the IRS started out with a $20 million valuation for a 15-percent interest in this company.[3] The taxpayer claimed in his return a value of about $2.5 million. By the time we got into court, the IRS outside value was down to about $6 million, and the taxpayer was still in the $2-2.5 million range. The IRS claimed the value was equal to the sum of the assets divided by the partnership interest. The court absolutely rejected that approach and came back to the value that was originally put on by the taxpayer, which was primarily an earnings-related valuation of a minority interest. The asset value is going to take on more importance for a controlling interest than for a minority interest.

There is a tendency for the courts to be more receptive to use of the discounted-cash-flow approach than they used to be. There is a case in which the court accepted a DCF approach.[4] In the *Weinberger* case, the court effectively broke open the Delaware Block Rule, and although they did not reject anything in this rule, they said all relevant approaches must be considered—one of which was a DCF approach.[5,6] Although the courts, in general, are more inclined to rely on market-based approaches, there is some trend toward more acceptance by the courts of DCF-type approaches.

[3]Estate of Martha B. Watts, 51 T.C.M. 60 (1985), appealed and affirmed, U.S. Court of Appeals, Eleventh Circuit, August 4, 1987.

[4]Las Vegas Dodge, Inc. v. United States, 85-2 U.S.T.C. Paragraph 9546 (1985).

[5]Weinberger v. UOP, Inc., 457 A.2d 701 (Del. Supr. 1983).

[6]In simplistic terms, the "Delaware Block Rule" accords a percentage weight, to be determined in each case, to the result of each of several approaches to value, most generally referred to as "investment value," "market value," and "asset value."

Discounts and Premia

Shannon P. Pratt, CFA

The issue of discounts and premia is very important in terms of money in business valuations. It is also one of the more difficult aspects of valuation. This is particularly true when partial interests rather than entire businesses are being valued. Not only is it a big money item, but it often tends to be very controversial and poorly understood.

Measuring Discounts and Premia: The Bases

Critical to the discussion of discounts or premia is the notion that they have no meaning whatsoever until their bases are defined. I have seen an incredible number of buy-sell agreements and appraisals written that refer to discounts or premia with no reference to the base from which those discounts or premia are to be taken. This is a typical error in business appraisal. The most common bases from which discounts or premia may be drawn are: freely marketable minority value, enterprise value assuming no changes, third party sale value, book value, and adjusted book value.

Freely marketable minority value, sometimes called the publicly traded equivalent value, is the price at which the fully registered shares would trade in a free and open market—i.e., the stock market value. It is the most commonly used base from which discounts for lack of marketability are deducted and the most common base to which premia for control are added.

Enterprise value is the value of the entire company. Unfortunately, this term is used differently by different people. Generally speaking, this value assumes no changes in the operation—in other words, business as usual. If the company is operating inefficiently, the assumption is that it will continue to operate inefficiently. Any potential synergies that may be achieved with the third-party buyer are not included in the enterprise value either. The value of the entire entity is usually as a going concern, assuming no major changes in capital structure or operations and no premia for synergistic values.

Third-party sale value is the value that could be realized in the sale of the company. Thus, it reflects the benefits of anticipated changes and synergies as a result of the relationship with the new owner, in contrast to the narrower definition of enterprise value, which does not.

Book value reflects the historical costs and the adjustments thereto, such as depreciation, and is not a measure of value *per se:* It is merely an accounting convention. Nevertheless, the book value is one number that is available in virtually every entity, and therefore it is often used as a basis from which discounts or premia are taken. When this is done, great caution must be exercised in the interpretation of the relevance of the book value base to some financial standard of value. Otherwise, applications of discounts or premia to a base that merely represents an accounting convention may have no economic significance in terms of current values, and these applications could render results meaningless and potentially misleading.

Adjusted book value is used in an almost infinite variety of ways to make the numbers more representative of some measure of value with meaningful economic significance.[1] Most commonly, the individual assets and liabilities are adjusted to more closely reflect current market values. Conceptually, this starting point for applying discounts or premia is more meaningful than just the accounting convention of book value as reported on a firm's financial statements. The usefulness of adjusted book value is influenced by the quality of the data available for the subject company and often the comparative companies.

It is also necessary to specify the level of ownership interest to which discounts or premia may be applied. That is, are the premia or discounts being applied only to the equity interest, or are they being applied to all of the invested capital? This would seem to be an obvious distinction, but it is often overlooked. I suggest that if a percentage premium applicable to equity were applied to all of the invested capital, the result in most cases will likely be an overvaluation of the market value of the total invested capital.

---

[1]See Mr. Nicholas's presentation, pp. 31-37, for a discussion of book value.

Minority Interest Discounts and Control Premia[2]

One of the most important variables affecting value is the degree of control rights (if any) inherent in the interest being valued. "Minority stock interests in a closed corporation are usually worth much less than the proportionate share of the assets to which they attach."[3] Fifty-five years after this was written, we are still recognizing that minority interests are usually worth less than a proportionate share of the total enterprise value. This revelation comes as a shock to many people who have always assumed that a partial interest is worth a *pro rata* portion of the value of the total enterprise.

The concepts of a minority-interest discount and a control premium may properly be thought of as shadow images of each other. As a generality, the base from which a minority-interest discount is taken would be some measure of the value of the enterprise as a whole. The American Society of Appraisers (ASA) has defined minority-interest discount as "the reduction from the *pro rata* share of the value of the entire business to reflect the absence of the power of control." Conversely, the base to which a control premium would be added normally would be some measure of minority-interest value. The ASA has defined a control premium as "the additional value inherent in the control interest, as contrasted with a minority interest that reflects its power of control." Using this definition, the minority-interest discount is the reverse of the control premium.

As law professors Fellows and Painter (1978) have pointed out, "a minority discount...is a corollary of a majority premium and depends on the latter for its validity." One must recognize, however, that the distinction between a controlling interest and a minority interest is not necessarily cut-and-dried; it may be only a matter of degree. The value of control depends on the ability to exercise any or all of the rights typically associated with control. Consequently, if control is an issue in the valuation, the analyst should assess the extent to which the various elements of control exist in the particular situation and consider the impact of each element on the value of control.

Exhibit 1 lists the prerogatives of control. It is apparent that the owner of a controlling interest in an enterprise enjoys some very valuable rights. Many factors, however, may limit a majority owner's

[2]Portions of this section are excerpted from Pratt (1989), Chapter 15.

[3]Cravens v. Welch, 10 Fed. Supp. 94 (1935).

EXHIBIT 1. Prerogatives of Control

1. Elect directors and appoint management.
2. Determine management compensation and perquisites.
3. Set policy and change the course of business.
4. Acquire or liquidate assets.
5. Select people with whom to do business and award contracts.
6. Make acquisitions.
7. Liquidate, dissolve, sell out, or recapitalize the company.
8. Sell or acquire Treasury shares.
9. Register the company's stock for a public offering.
10. Declare and pay dividends.
11. Change the articles of incorporation or bylaws.

Source: Shannon P. Pratt

right or ability to exercise many of the prerogatives normally associated with control, thus limiting the value accruing to the control position. For example, certain types of companies, such as insurance or utility companies, may be very difficult—if not impossible—to liquidate within a short period of time.

There are several factors that affect the degree of control of majority shareholders.

1. *Cumulative versus noncumulative voting.* If the company has noncumulative voting with respect to the election of directors, the whole pie belongs to the majority. If the company has cumulative voting, some of the value attributable to the ability to elect directors will shift from the majority holder to the minority holders.

2. *Contractual restrictions.* Many typical control rights may be denied to a company through contractual restrictions, such as indenture provisions in conjunction with a debt obligation, which may prevent dividend payments, increased management compensation, liquidation of assets, acquisitions, or changes in the direction of the business.

3. *Effect of regulation.* Government regulation of operations may limit the controlling owner's ability to exercise prerogatives.

4. *Financial condition of business.* Many of the rights associated with control are rendered of little value economically simply because of the company's financial condition. These could include the right to decide on management compensation, dividends, stock or asset purchases, or acquisition of other companies.

5. *Effect of state statutes.* Statutes affecting the respective rights of controlling and minority stockholders vary from state to state. In about half the states, a simple majority can approve major actions such as a merger, sale, liquidation, or recapitalization of the company. Other states require a majority of two-thirds or greater to approve such actions, which means that a minority of just over one-third (or less in a few states) has the power to block such actions. The variations in state law concerning minority-stockholder rights can have an important bearing on the valuation.

6. *Effect of distribution of ownership.* If one person owns 49 percent of the stock and another person owns 51 percent, the 49-percent holder has little or no positive control—and in many states may not even have the "negative control" of being able to block certain actions. If two stockholders own 49 percent each, however, and a third stockholder owns 2 percent, the 2 percent stockholder—because of his swing vote power—may be able to command a considerable premium over a *pro rata* portion of the value of the total company for that particular block of stock.

Equal individual interests normally are worth less than a *pro rata* portion of what the total enterprise would be worth. If each of three stockholders or partners owns a one-third interest, no one has complete control. No one is in a relatively inferior position, either, unless two of the three stockholders have close ties with each other that the third does not share. In this case, the sum of the values of the individual interests usually is less than what the total enterprise could be sold for to a single buyer, and the percentage discount from *pro rata* value for each equal interest normally will be lower than that for a minority interest that has no control whatsoever.

In summary, each situation must be analyzed individually with respect to the degree of control (or lack of it). When any control element is lacking, any value attributable to control must be diminished accordingly. If there is any significant element of control present in a minority interest, that value also should be recognized.

Closely related to the matter of controlling interest versus minority interest is the matter of voting rights (or lack thereof). Voting rights constitute one of the most difficult variables to quantify in terms of impact on value. In general, the greater the extent to which the issue of control is involved, the greater the importance of voting rights in terms of value. For extremely small minority interests, the market accords very little value to voting rights. Where swing votes or majority interests are involved, the impact on value may be significant. So, the issue of voting versus nonvoting stock is something that must be analyzed in conjunction with the distribution of ownership.

Control Premium Studies

There are two broad sources of data for quantifying the amount of a minority discount or control premium: control premium studies and data from trust and estate sales. The thousands of daily transactions on the stock exchange are, of course, minority-interest transactions. Each year, a controlling interest in a few hundred of these public companies is purchased—in almost all cases at a price representing a premium over the market price at which the stock had traded as a minority interest. Several services follow these acquisitions and publish data on control premia. One of these is the *Mergerstat Review* published by the W.T. Grimm Company (now a subsidiary of the Merrill Lynch Business Brokerage & Valuation, Inc.).

Table 1 shows the percentage premium paid over the market price from 1968 to 1988. The median is probably a better measure than the arithmetic average, because the arithmetic average is driven up by a few very large percentage premia. Note the relation between the control premium and the level of the market, as proxied by the Dow Jones Industrial Average (DJIA). If you think the stock market is efficient, you may be somewhat convinced, by looking at these data, that the merger market is more efficient than the stock market. That is, the merger market may be more comprehensive than the stock market in collecting, analyzing, and factoring into pricing all relevant data bearing on value. In 1974, for example, the stock market hit a low of 577, and the average control premium hit its high of 50.1 percent. Notice also that the pattern in the control premia from 1980 through 1988 started around 49 percent. Then, as the market got very high, culminating in the first three quarters of 1987 (prior to the stock market drop), the premia were at their lowest levels; after the stock market dropped, they started back up again.

Table 2 translates the average premium paid into the implied minority-interest discount (which was computed on the average, rather than on the median).

There are also a number of acquisitions in the

TABLE 1. Percent Premium Paid Over Market Price (1968-1988)

Year	DJIA High	DJIA Low	Average	Median	Base*
1968	985.21	825.13	25.1	N/A	271
1969	968.85	769.93	25.7	N/A	191
1970	842.00	631.16	33.4	N/A	80
1971	950.82	797.97	33.1	N/A	74
1972	1,036.27	889.15	33.8	N/A	93
1973	1,051.70	788.31	44.5	N/A	145
1974	891.66	577.60	50.1	43.1	147
1975	881.81	632.04	41.4	30.1	129
1976	1,014.79	858.71	40.4	31.1	168
1977	999.75	800.85	40.9	36.2	218
1978	907.74	742.12	46.2	41.5	240
1979	897.61	796.67	49.9	47.6	229
1980	1,000.17	759.13	49.9	44.6	169
1981	1,024.05	824.01	48.0	41.9	166
1982	1,070.55	776.92	47.4	43.5	176
1983	1,287.20	1,027.04	37.7	34.0	168
1984	1,286.64	1,086.57	37.9	34.4	199
1985	1,553.10	1,184.96	37.1	27.7	331
1986	1,955.60	1,502.30	38.2	29.9	333
1987	2,722.42	1,738.74	38.3	30.8	237
1988	2,183.50	1,879.14	41.9	30.9	410

* Base: The number of transactions where a premium over market was paid. Premia can only be calculated on acquisitions of publicly traded companies.

Source: Mergerstat Review 1988. (Schaumburg, IL: Merrill Lynch Business Brokerage & Valuation, Inc. 1989.)

public markets where minority interests—not controlling interests—were acquired. **Table 3** shows that the premia paid for minority-interest acquisitions were not as great as for controlling-interest acquisitions from 1982 to 1986. In 1987 and 1988, this was not the case. Part of the problem may be that this is a small database with considerably more control transactions than minority-interest transactions.

Table 4 shows the median premium paid relative to the seller's price/earnings (P/E) ratio. Where the P/E ratio is higher in the public market, there is a tendency for the control premium percentage to be lower—unless the P/E ratios are relatively high because the earnings base was abnormally low. In other words, generally there is a smaller control premium for companies that already had a higher P/E ratio in the public market.

Public companies tend to be acquired at considerably higher price/earnings ratios on average than private companies that are acquired. **Table 5** shows the median P/E ratio paid for acquisitions of public

and private companies from 1980 to 1988. The data show a consistent relationship, and there are a variety of reasons for this. One is that a public-company acquirer may want to avoid dilution and therefore is not willing to pay more than the P/E on his own company. Another reason is that a private company does not have the same degree of exposure to the acquisition market that a public company does. Public companies are listed in many computerized and published data sources; private companies are not as easy to find. In addition, the accounting data for private companies may not be as good as the data for public companies; consequently, there may be more risk in acquiring them. Finally, there is more liquidity in the shares of publicly held companies than in the shares of privately held companies.

Houlihan, Lokey, Howard & Zukin, Inc. conducted an industry-wide control premium study. Some of their results are summarized in Figures 1 and 2. **Figure 1** shows the trailing 12-month median control premium from the first quarter of 1987

TABLE 2. W. T. Grimm Control Premia

Year of Buyout	Number of Transactions	Average Premium Paid Over Market[a] (%)	Median Premium Paid (%)	Implied Interest Discount[b] (%)
1980	169	49.9	44.6	33.3
1981	166	48.0	41.9	32.4
1982	176	47.4	43.5	32.2
1983	168	37.7	34.0	27.4
1984	199	37.9	34.4	27.5
1985	331	37.1	27.7	27.1
1986	333	38.2	29.9	27.6
1987	237	38.3	30.8	27.7

Notes:

[a] The premium paid over market is a percentage based on the buyout price over the market price of the seller's stock five business days prior to the announcement date.

[b] Formula: $1 - (1 \div (1 + \text{Average Premium Paid})$.
For example: $1 - (1 \div 1.499) = 1 - 0.667 = 0.333$.

Source: Mergerstat Review 1987. (Schaumburg, IL: Merrill Lynch Business Brokerage & Valuation, Inc. 1988.) Discount calculated by Willamette Management Associates, Inc.

through the first quarter of 1989. These control premia were lower in the first three quarters of 1987, when the stock market was very high just prior to the October 1987 stock market correction. Obviously, many of the potential acquirers thought at that time that the market was at an unsustainably high level. Indeed, it did make an appropriate correction. **Figure 2** shows the 12-month median control premia by industry as of March 31, 1989.

Trust and Estate Sales

The second source of information on minority-interest discounts and control premia is trust and estate sales. H. Calvin Coolidge, a bank trust officer

responsible for administering trusts and estates that owned all or portions of closely held businesses, compiled data on actual sale prices of closely held businesses.

In his first study, Coolidge (1975) compiled data on 30 actual sales of minority interests. He found that the average transaction price was 36 percent below book value and concluded with the following observations:

Only 20 percent of the sales were made at discounts less than 20 percent. A little more than half the sales (53-1/3 percent) were made at discounts that ranged from 22 percent to 48 percent, and 23-1/3 percent of the sales were made at discounts of from 54.4 percent to 78 percent. It would be dangerous to draw too many general-

TABLE 3. Average Percent Premium Paid: Controlling Versus Minority (1982-88)

	1982	Base*	1983	Base	1984	Base	1985	Base	1986	Base	1987	Base	1988	Base
Controlling Interest	48.5	165	37.8	160	39.0	191	37.3	310	39.1	308	38.2	228	41.9	402
Minority Interest	29.6	11	35.9	8	16.8	8	34.2	21	27.2	25	39.8	9	58.9	8

* Base: Number of transactions where a price was reported and a premium over market was paid.

Source: Mergerstat Review 1988. (Schaumburg, IL: Merrill Lynch Business Brokerage & Valuation, Inc. 1989.)

TABLE 4. Median Percent Premium Paid for Various Seller's P/E (1984-88)

Seller's P/E Ratio Five Days Before Announcement	1984	Base*	1985	Base	1986	Base	1987	Base	1988	Base
Deficit**	42.6	32	28.8	78	34.8	82	31.0	68	31.7	99
1.0 = 5.0X	50.1	6	80.0	18	100.0	1	21.4	1	40.4	2
5.1 - 8.0	37.8	29	32.0	36	13.3	4	17.5	5	50.4	32
8.1 - 10.0	35.6	28	28.2	45	26.7	12	46.0	6	36.0	36
10.1 - 12.0	31.6	21	27.3	41	16.6	15	17.5	5	31.8	43
12.1 - 15.0	33.8	33	24.2	45	17.4	28	26.1	21	25.2	40
Over 15.0	28.1	50	23.3	68	31.9	180	33.1	118	27.3	122

* Base: Number of transactions where a premium over market was paid and a P/E calculated.

** Companies operating at a deficit when acquired.

Source: Mergerstat Review 1988. (Schaumburg, IL: Merrill Lynch Business Brokerage & Valuation, Inc. 1989.)

izations from the survey, but those sales where the discounts were below 20 percent involved, with one exception, purchases from close relatives where friendly relations existed. The exception was the sale by a holder of swing shares who used his leverage well, but still took a 4.3 percent discount. At the other end of the spectrum was the settlement of a three year bitter dispute between two families; the majority family raised its token offer only after threat of a lawsuit, but the price the minority interest took nonetheless represented a 78 percent discount.[4] An update published in 1983 indicates that there is a trend toward even higher discounts when disposing of minority interests in closely held corporations. That study found a much higher concentration of discounts from book value at the high end of the range. The average discount for the two studies combined was approximately 40 percent. The updated study concludes as follows.

Each of the sales used in the survey involved a combination of factors that made it somewhat unique. To use any of the data, or any classification of the data, as definitive proof of the discount to be applied in a prospective valuation would be dangerous. This should not, however, obscure the true significance of the data, which is that in the actual marketplace, the typical discount is not of token size, but of substantial magnitude.[5]

Discounts for Lack of Marketability[6]

The distinction between a minority-interest discount and a discount for lack of marketability is not always clear. Some writers and appraisers fail to distinguish

TABLE 5. Median P/E Paid: Public Versus Private Firms (1980-88)

	Acquisitions of Public Companies (Base*)	Acquisitions of Private Companies (Base*)
1980	11.5 (162)	10.3 (81)
1981	14.0 (160)	11.5 (70)
1982	12.8 (150)	10.1 (43)
1983	15.5 (141)	11.5 (48)
1984	15.1 (183)	11.4 (63)
1985	16.4 (240)	12.3 (187)
1986	24.3 (259)	16.5 (105)
1987	21.7 (191)	15.2 (25)
1988	18.3 (309)	12.8 (50)

* Base: Number of transactions disclosing P/E paid.

Source: Mergerstat Review 1988. (Schaumburg, IL: Merrill Lynch Business Brokerage & Valuation, Inc. 1989.)

[4]Coolidge (1975).

[5]Coolidge (1983).

[6]Portions of ths section are excerpted from Pratt (1989), Chapter 10, "Data on Discounts for Lack of Marketability."

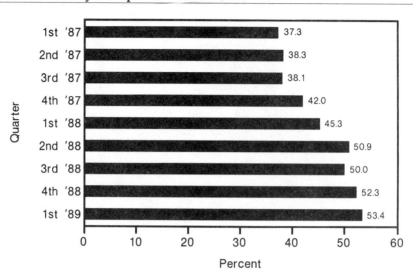

* Each premium shown above represents a trailing 12 month period.

Source: Houlihan, Lokey, Howard & Zukin, Inc., *Control Premium Study* (1989).

between the two discounts, but they are, in fact, two different—but interrelated—concepts. The concept of a minority-interest discount reflects the relation between the interest being valued and the total enterprise. The primary factor bearing on the value of the minority interest is the degree of control. The concept of marketability relates to the degree of liquidity—how quickly and how certainly an investment may be converted to cash. The interrelation stems largely from the fact that minority interests tend to suffer to a greater degree from lack of marketability than do controlling interests.

Many factors affect the relative marketability of different business interests. One factor is the size of the interest. In some cases, a smaller block would be easier to market than a larger block, and in other cases the reverse would be true. The importance of the marketability factor in business valuation has been gaining increasing recognition over the years. There is considerable evidence suggesting that the discount for the lack-of-marketability factor alone for a closely held stock compared with a publicly traded counterpart should average between 35 and 50 percent. This is compared to freely tradeable public minority interests.

Because interests in closely held businesses, by definition, do not enjoy the ready market of a publicly traded stock, a share in a private company is usually worth less than an otherwise-comparable share in a publicly held company. Even a controlling interest in a private company suffers to some extent

from lack of marketability. It usually takes at least a few months to sell a company—sometimes considerably longer. The relation between the discount for lack of marketability and the discount for a minority interest lies in the fact that even after discounting a minority interest for its lack of control, it is usually still harder to sell a minority interest than to sell a controlling interest in a closely held business.

Many court decisions, especially those involving valuations for gift- and estate-tax purposes, have taken a single lump-sum discount to reflect marketability, minority interest, and sometimes other factors. Conceptual thinking in the valuation exercise, however, usually may be more precise to the extent that it is possible to isolate and quantify the various valuation factors, especially the more important ones. Fortunately, in recent years both valuation practitioners and courts have been giving separate recognition to the impact of minority-interest and marketability factors. A 1982 estate-tax decision articulated the distinction between the minority and marketability discounts very clearly:

In their arguments, neither the practitioner nor respondent clearly focuses on the fact that two conceptually distinct discounts are involved here, one for lack of marketability and the other for lack of control. The minority shareholder discount is designed to reflect the decreased value of shares that do not convey control of a closely held corporation. The lack of marketability discount, on the other hand, is designed to reflect the fact that there is no ready market for shares in a closely held corporation. Although there may be some overlap between these two discounts in that lack of control may reduce marketability, it should be borne in mind that even controlling shares in a nonpublic corporation suffer from lack of marketability because of the absence of a ready private placement market and the fact that flotation costs would have to be incurred if the corporation were to publicly offer its stock.[7]

If a minority interest in a closely held business is valued by reference to day-to-day trading prices of publicly held stocks, minority interests are being compared with other minority interests. The closely-held-stock value should be discounted for marketability with respect to the publicly held stock, but not for minority interest.

If a minority interest in a closely held business is being valued by capitalization of earnings, book value, or some other approach without comparison to daily trading prices of publicly held stocks, and if the capitalization rates or multiples employed are applicable to controlling interests, discounts may be appropriate to reflect both the lack of marketability and the minority interest. It is not uncommon to find a minority interest valued at 35 percent or less of the stock's underlying net asset value, reflecting both the minority-interest and lack-of-marketability factors.

Conversely, if a controlling interest in a closely held business is being valued with reference to day-to-day trading prices of publicly held stocks, which are minority interests, it may be appropriate to add a premium for control. Occasionally, it works out that the discount for lack of marketability in a privately held company more or less offsets the premium for control. One possible explanation for this is that public companies tend to be reluctant to incur dilution by paying a higher P/E ratio for acquisitions than the price at which their own stock is selling. In effect, a controlling stockholder of a closely held company who sells to a public company is giving up control but gaining liquidity. (The degree of liquidity gained will depend, of course, on the extent to which the seller gets cash, freely tradeable public securities, restricted securities, or some other consideration.) Apart from other valuation factors, in some cases these two factors by themselves have the net effect of canceling each other out. In cases where the value of control versus the disadvantage of lack of liquidity do not offset each other, the scale usually tips in favor of the former when the interest being valued has all the benefits of control. When the

interest being valued holds a small majority but does not have all the rights of control, the scale may very well be tipped in favor of the disadvantage of lack of liquidity.

Marketability Discount Studies

There are three sources of information on the discounts for lack of marketability: studies of restricted stocks, studies of private transactions prior to public offerings, and studies of costs of flotation.

Restricted-Stock Studies. The data on restricted stocks—that is, stocks of public corporations that are not registered for public trading (restricted shares for one reason or another)—provide a good source of information on the lack-of-marketability discounts. These shares often change hands in private placements, so one may compare the private placement price to the day-to-day trading price. The percentage difference is a proxy for the discount for lack of marketability.

1. *SEC Institutional Investor Study.*[8] In a major study of institutional investor actions, the SEC examined the amount of discount at which transactions in restricted stock (letter stock) took place compared to the prices of identical but unrestricted stock on the open market. **Table 6** shows the amounts of these discounts for the years 1966 through 1969, categorized by the market in which the restricted stock trades. I call your attention to the over-the-counter nonreporting companies. As you know, a company may trade over the counter through the pink sheets and be a nonreporting company if it has either less than $1 million worth of assets or less than 500 stockholders. These companies would be most analogous to most closely held companies. Note that the preponderance of transactions among these companies took place at discounts of between 30 and 40 percent from their publicly traded stock counterparts. These are private transactions in publicly traded stocks that are equivalent in all respects to the freely tradeable public stock—voting, dividends, all other rights—except for the fact that they have restrictions on their trading.

[7]Estate of Woodbury G. Andrews, 79 T.C. 938 (1982).

[8]U.S. Congress. House. "Discounts Involved in Purchases of Common Stock (1966-1969)." *Institutional Investor Study Report of the Securities and Exchange Commission.* H.R. Doc. No. 64, Part 5, 92d Cong., 1st Sess. (1971), pp. 2444-56.

TABLE 6. SEC Institutional Investor Study: Discount by Trading Market

	Discount: -15.0% to 0.0%		Discount: 0.1% to 10.0%		Discount: 10.1% to 20.0%		Discount: 20.1% to 30.0%	
	No. of Trans-actions	Value of Purchases (Dollars)	No. of Trans-actions	Value of Purchases (Dollars)	No. of Trans-actions	Value of Purchases (Dollars)	No. of Trans-actions	Value of Purchases (Dollars)
Trading Market								
Unknown	1	$ 1,500,000	2	$ 2,496,583	1	$ 205,000	—	$ —
NYSE	7	3,760,663	13	15,111,798	13	24,503,988	10	17,954,085
ASE	2	7,263,060	4	15,850,000	11	14,548,750	20	46,200,677
OTC (Reporting Co.)	11	13,828,757	39	13,613,676	35	38,585,259	30	35,479,946
OTC (Nonreporting Co.)	5	8,329,369	9	5,265,925	18	25,122,024	17	11,229,155
(Total	26	$34,681,849	67	$52,337,982	78	$102,965,021	77	$110,863,863

	Discount: 30.1% to 40.0%		Discount: 0.1% to 50.0%		Discount: 50.1% to 80.0%		Total	
	No. of Trans-actions	Value of Purchases (Dollars)	No. of Trans-actions	Value of Purchases (Dollars)	No. of Trans-actions	Value of Purchases (Dollars)	No. of Trans-actions	Value of Purchases (Dollars)
Trading Market								
Unknown	2	$ 3,332,000	—	$ —	1	$ 1,259,995	7	$ 8,793,578
NYSE	3	11,102,501	1	1,400,000	4	5,005,068	51	78,838,103
ASE	7	21,074,298	1	44,250	4	4,802,404	49	109,783,439
OTC (Reporting Co.)	30	38,689,328	13	9,284,047	21	8,996,406	179	178,477,419
OTC (Nonreporting Co.)	25	29,423,584	20	11,377,431	18	13,505,545	112	104,253,033
Total	67	$103,621,711	35	$22,105,728	48	$33,569,418	398	$480,145,572

Source: U.S. Congress. House. "Discounts Involved in Purchases of Common Stock (1966-1969)." *Institutional Investor Study Report of the Securities and Exchange Commission.* H.R. Doc. No. 64, Part 5, 92d Cong., 1st Sess. (1971), pp. 2444-56.

2. ***Gelman Study.*** Gelman (1972) studied prices paid for restricted securities by four closed-end investment companies specializing in restricted-securities investments. **Table 7** summarizes the results of this study. From 89 transactions between 1968 and 1970, Gelman found that both the arithmetic average and median discounts were 33 percent and that almost 60 percent of the purchases were at discounts of 30 percent and higher.

3. ***Moroney Study.*** Moroney (1973) explored the prices of 146 transactions in restricted securities by 10 registered investment companies (see **Table 8**). This is the most comprehensive study since the SEC Institutional Investor Study. Moroney was the pioneer in making the restricted-stock studies widely used by investment analysts for the purpose of quantifying discounts for lack of marketability and was instrumental in getting these discounts recognized by the courts.

4. ***Summary of Results.*** **Table 9** is a summary of the conclusions of the major restricted-stock studies. The results of these studies are remarkably consistent, considering the long time span and the different methods. The average discount is about 30 to 35 percent.

Studies on Private Transactions Prior to Public Offerings. The second source of information on lack-of-marketability discounts is the set of studies on private transactions prior to public offerings. Private placements of stocks that already have an established market benefit from established marketability once restrictions on public trading of the specific subject shares are lifted. Logically, one would think that the discount for lack of marketability for shares in a closely held company would be even greater than the discounts on publicly traded shares because they have no potential public market—or at least no assured potential public market—and may never have one. The transactions in closely held shares held prior to the establishment of a public market support this thesis.

1. **Robert W. Baird & Co. Studies.** John Emory (1985) conducted two studies on private transactions within the five to six months prior to an initial public offering. The first study covered stocks of companies that had successful public offerings between January 1, 1980 and June 30, 1981. The second study covered stocks of companies that went public between January 1, 1985 and June 30, 1986. In his first study, he found that the average discount on these private transactions of closely held companies prior to a public offering took place

TABLE 7. Gelman Study Results

Size of Discount (%)	Number of Common Stocks	Percent of Total
Less than 15.0	5	6
15.0 - 19.9	9	10
20.0 - 24.9	13	15
25.0 - 29.9	9	10
30.0 - 34.9	12	13
35.0 - 39.9	9	10
40.0 and over	32	36
Total	89	100

Source: Gelman (1972:354).

TABLE 8. Moroney: Original Purchase Discounts for Restricted Stocks

Investment Company	Original Purchase Discount*	Number of Blocks
Bayrock Growth Fund, Inc., New York City (formerly Fla. Growth Fund)	Blocks bought at discounts of 12% to 66%	4
Diebold Venture Capital Corp., New York City	Blocks bought at discounts of 16% to 50%	6
Enterprise Fund, Inc., Los Angeles	Blocks bought at discounts of 31% to 87%	10
Harbor Fund, Inc., Los Angeles	Block bought at a discount of 62%	1
Inventure Capital Corp., Boston	At acquisition dates, all blocks were valued at cost	
Mates Investment Fund, Inc., New York City	Block bought at a discount of 62%	1
New America Fund, Inc., Los Angeles (formerly Fund of Letters, Inc.)	Blocks bought at discounts of 3% to 58%	32
Price Capital Corp., New York City	Blocks bought at discounts of 15% to 52%	7
SMC Investment Corp., Los Angeles	Blocks bought at 30% premium, discounts of 4% to 78%	12
Value Line Development Capital Corp., New York City	Blocks bought at discounts of 10% to 90%	35
Value Line Special Situations Fund, Inc., New York City	Blocks bought at discounts of 10% to 81%	38

Note:

*Discounts are from the quoted market value of the same corporation's "free" stock of the same class.

Source: Moroney (1973).

TABLE 9. Summary of Restricted-Stock Studies

Study	Years Covered in Study	Average Discount (%)
SEC Overall Average[a]	1966-1969	25.8
SEC Nonreporting OTC Companies[a]	1966-1969	32.6
Gelman[b]	1968-1970	33.0
Trout[c]	1968-1972	33.5[i]
Moroney[d]	See footnote [h]	35.6
Maher[e]	1969-1973	35.4
Standard Research Consultants[f]	1978-1982	45.0[i]
Willamette Management Assoc., Inc.[g]	1981-1984	31.2[i]

Notes:

[a] From "Discounts Involved in Purchases of Common Stock (1966-1969)," *Institutional Investor Study Report of the Securities and Exchange Commission.* H.R. Doc. No. 64, Part 5, 92d Cong., 1st Sess. 1971, pp. 2444-2456.

[b] From Milton Gelman, "An Economist-Financial Analyst's Approach to Valuing Stock of a Closely Held Company," *Journal of Taxation*, June 1972, pp. 353-354.

[c] From Robert R. Trout, "Estimation of the Discount Associated with the Transfer of Restricted Securities," *Taxes*, June 1977, pp. 381-385.

[d] From Robert E. Moroney, "Most Courts Overvalue Closely Held Stocks," *Taxes*, March 1973, pp. 144-154.

[e] From J. Michael Maher, "Discounts for Lack of Marketability for Closely-Held Business Interests," Taxes, September 1976, pp. 562-571.

[f] From "Revenue Ruling 77-287 Revisited," *SRC Quarterly Reports*, Spring 1983, pp. 1-3.

[g] From Willamette Management Associates study (unpublished).

[h] Although the years covered in this study are likely to be 1969-1972, no specific years were given in the published account.

[i] Median discounts.

Source: Pratt (1989:248).

at a 60-percent average and 66-percent median discount from the price at which they ultimately went public. In the updated study, the average discount was about 43 percent. The discounts were higher than those shown by letter stock.

2. ***Willamette Management Associates Studies.*** Willamette conducted a series of studies on the prices of private stock transactions relative to those of subsequent public offerings of stock of the same companies. The results of these studies are summarized in **Table 10**. As shown, the average discounts varied from period to period, but in all cases they were higher than the average discounts shown in the studies for restricted stocks of companies that already had an established public-trading market—which is the result one would expect. We are finding that the average discounts in the most recent years are about 43 percent. I think that 43 percent is a reasonable point of departure for dis-

counts for lack of marketability for minority shares in privately held companies compared to publicly traded stocks.

Keep in mind that you do not necessarily have to decide what the enterprise value is to value a minority interest in a privately held company. In cases such as *Gallo*[9] and *Hallmark,*[10] as well as many others dealing with minority interest, the question of enterprise value was never addressed. We considered the question of comparative publicly traded stocks, which are already minority interests; and then, from that, we took a marketability discount.

Cost of Flotation. Finally, the cost of flotation is sometimes used as a proxy for measuring the discount for lack of marketability for valuing controlling interests. Results of the most comprehensive study on this subject, conducted by the SEC between

[9]Estate of Mark S. Gallo, 50 T.C.M 470 (1985).

[10]Estate of Joyce C. Hall, 92 T.C. No. 19 (1989).

TABLE 10. Summary of Discounts for Private Transaction P/E Ratios
Compared to Public Offering P/E Ratios Adjusted for Changes
in Industry P/E Ratios

Time Period	Number of Companies Analyzed	Number of Transactions Analyzed	Median Discount (%)
1975-78	20	34	49.6
1979	9	17	62.9
1980-82	58	113	55.5
1984	20	33	74.4
1985	18	25	41.7
1986	47	74	47.5
1987	25	40	43.3

Source: Willamette Management Associates, Inc.

1971 and 1972, are shown in **Table 11**. For any current situation, a study should be done on costs of flotation of companies comparable to the subject company in size and other characteristics. As a broad generality, costs of flotation tend to be higher today than those shown in Table 11.

Other Discounts

There are several other discounts related to valuing closely held companies. Three are of particular interest: blockage, key-person discount, and portfolio discount. The discount for lack of voting rights is not usually very great if you are comparing it to small minority voting interests.

Blockage is a term applicable to large blocks of publicly traded stock. If the size is large relative to normal trading volume, it may be necessary for the seller to accept a discount from the current market quote to induce a block trader to take down the entire position. Blockage is not applicable as a concept in private securities, although it may be applicable when it comes to thinly traded securities.

The *key-person discount* is for the loss of a key person in a company. Rob Oliver pointed out that there have been several recent estate-tax cases in which a discount for loss of the key person has been as high as 25 percent. (See pp. 4-12).

The *portfolio discount* is for the fact that even in purchasing a controlling interest, there is some disadvantage—to at least the typical purchaser—in

TABLE 11. Cost of Flotation

Size of Issue (Millions)	Number	Compensation (Percent of Gross Proceeds)	Other Expense (Percent of Gross Proceeds)
Under 0.5	43	13.24	10.35
0.5 - 0.99	227	12.48	8.26
1.00 - 1.99	271	10.60	5.87
2.00 - 4.99	450	8.19	3.71
5.00 - 9.99	287	6.70	2.03
10.00 - 19.99	170	5.52	1.11
20.00 - 49.99	109	4.41	0.62
50.00 - 99.99	30	3.94	0.31
100.00 - 499.99	12	3.03	0.16
Over 500.00	0	—	—
Total/Averages	1,599	8.41	4.02

Source: Cost of Flotation of Registered Issues 1971-72. Washington, D.C.: Securities and Exchange Commission (1974:9).

FIGURE 2.   Control Premia by Industry (12-Month Control Premia)*

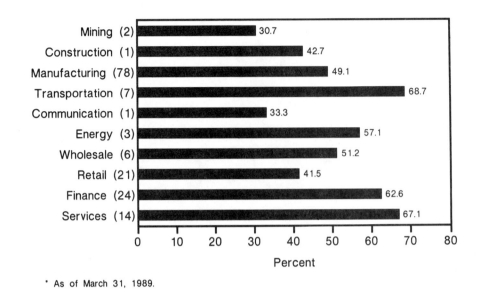

* As of March 31, 1989.

Source: Houlihan, Lokey, Howard & Zukin, Inc., *Control Premium Study* (1989).

buying a portfolio of dissimilar or unrelated assets. This discount applies to companies that are in multiple lines of business rather than single lines. If one looks at the P/E ratios of conglomerates, for example, compared to the blended P/E ratios of the various industries that make up those companies in the conglomerate, one will generally find that the market accords a discount of about 15 percent to conglomerates. That is one way that the so-called portfolio discount might be quantified.

Conclusion

For discounts or premia to have conceptual meaning and be susceptible to quantification, the base to which they are to be applied must be defined exactly. Discounts for minority interest (compared to enterprise value or third-party sale value of the entire company) and discounts for lack of marketability (compared to fully registered and actively traded public stocks) are two separate concepts—although they are interrelated. Together, these two discounts frequently cumulate to a total of over 50 percent from a *pro rata* share of the price at which an entire company should be sold. Because the magnitudes of premia and discounts may be so substantial, it is important to be familiar with the extensive empirical evidence available when attempting to quantify premia or discounts in any particular situation.

Question and Answer Session

Question: Can a discount for lack of marketability be justified for a controlling interest? How should this discount be measured?

Pratt: Often people use the cost of floating an issue as a proxy for the discount for lack of marketability in the case of the minority shareholder. This is an incorrect use. The flotation cost is absolutely irrelevant because a minority-interest holder cannot force a public offering—unless, of course, he has some kind of contractual right to do so. Consequently, flotation costs are not the proper measure by which to quantify discounts for lack of marketability for a minority interest. Cost of flotation provides relevant empirical data for quantifying the discount for lack of marketability in the case of a controlling interest. Alternatively, one might consider merger and acquisition fees, legal and accounting costs, and other costs incidental to selling a company.

Question: Can a control premium and a lack-of-marketability discount be applied to the same stock?

Pratt: Yes, in some cases. The control premium will probably be larger, however. For example, if the control premium increases the value of the shares above the value of the publicly traded equivalent minority-interest value, the discount for lack of marketability will probably not reduce the value back to the publicly traded equivalent—although it could.

Question: Should an Employee Stock Ownership Plan (ESOP) shareholder expect some discount for marketability compared to publicly traded shares?

Pratt: Yes, but a discount is not a certainty. Some appraisers do not take a discount for lack of marketability on the grounds that there is no need for one because of the put option in the ESOP. The Department of Labor eschews that position; it does not require a discount for lack of marketability, but it does require that appraisers analyze all the facts and circumstances in making a determination as to whether a discount for lack of marketability is merited for a particular ESOP situation.

At Willamette, we have occasionally valued ESOPs with no discount for lack of marketability. More commonly, however, we do have a discount for lack of marketability; it ranges from 5 to 25 percent.

The Department of Labor has been working on new regulations for the valuation of ESOP shares. One of the things that will be addressed is the question of the discount for lack of marketability for ESOP shares.

Question: Will the minority-interest discount be different if the stock is held by the family rather than held by somebody else?

Pratt: In 1981 the Internal Revenue Service issued Revenue Ruling 81-253, the Family Attribution Ruling, on whether a minority-interest discount could be taken on a gift of a minority-interest position when other family members held a controlling interest in the company. The ruling indicates that a minority discount cannot be taken in this situation. Keep in mind, however, that revenue rulings are not law; they merely represent the regulatory authority's interpretation of the law. This question has been tested in court time after time (starting with the *Bright* case,[12] going on through the *Propstra* case,[13] the *Andrews* case,[14] and many others). The plaintiffs lost every time it was tested in court. The fair-market-value concept is consistently interpreted by the courts to mean the price at which the property would trade between a *hypothetical* willing buyer and willing seller, not between any *particular* willing buyer and willing seller. Therefore, the fact that the person who is giving or receiving the minority stock is related to the control holder is irrelevant in the eyes of the court, and the stock is to be valued as if the transaction is taking place on an arms-length basis between unrelated people.

Question: In the studies you discussed, how much of the control premium is firm-specific and how much results from gains due to increased synergy?

Pratt: There is no way to separate the two forces. Obviously, these control premia represent a combination of a lower discount rate—if there is one—for a controlling interest, plus perceived gains from increased synergies.

Question: Please discuss the value of employee

[12]Estate of Bright v. United States, 658 F. 2d 999 (1981).

[13]Propstra v. United States, 680 F. 2d 1248 (1981).

[14]Estate of Woodbury G. Andrews, 79 T.C. 938 (1982).

agreements, with particular reference to buy-sell agreements and restrictive covenants.

Pratt: Restrictive covenants most likely reduce the value of shares by requiring an increase in the discount for lack of marketability. For example, if an employee agreement contains a covenant that requires the employee to offer the shares back to the company 90 days before the shares can be sold to an outsider, the marketability of the shares is reduced significantly. This type of clause will inhibit the employee's ability to sell to an outsider, because very few people are going to make an offer and then hold it open for 90 days while people inside the company think about whether they want to exercise their right of first refusal.

Buy-sell agreements may or may not be binding when it comes to estate-tax valuations. To be binding, they must have been entered into at a fair market value, at arms length, and they must be binding both during life and death. More restrictive provisions were put into the recent tax laws, but even those requirements will not, for the most part, make a buy-sell agreement value-binding in the case of an estate-tax valuation.

Question: What is the value of minority shares with no dividend and no apparent chance of liquidity?

Pratt: There may be extreme cases in which the stock could be valueless. Obviously, the value depends on what the stockholder is going to get. To the extent that dividends are paid, the discount for lack of marketability may be less because the stockholder is receiving money; he does not have to sell the security to receive cash. For that reason, the discounts for lack of marketability for debt instruments and for dividend-paying preferred stocks are substantially less than the discounts for lack of marketability for most common stocks. Because of the interest or dividend payments, the marketability does not make as much difference. The greater the dividend on the stock, the less the discount for marketability. If a stock has never paid a dividend and is not liquid—that is, there is no way to get cash—one might make a case that the security is worthless. I have a client who would take 10 percent of book value for his stock; it has never paid a dividend, and the company will not even offer him that much to redeem the stock.

Question: If the minority-interest discount is a corollary of the control premium, aren't both of them affected by the size of the minority interest?

Pratt: Yes. To the extent that the minority interest begins to have control features, the minority-interest discount would tend to be less.

Question: Do any states currently permit a minority shareholder to be squeezed out without compensation in the event of a liquidation or recapitalization?

Pratt: No, I do not think so. At least 46 of the states have dissenting-stockholder rights; all 50 probably do. Most dissenting-stockholder-rights laws require that a minority stockholder who is squeezed out must be made "whole." In other words, a dissenting minority stockholder has dissenting-stockholder appraisal rights, which are exercised in various ways in the different states. Usually, the minority stockholder receives a pay-out of the "fair value" of his stock, which is interpreted very differently in most situations from fair market value. That does not mean, though, that the dissenting stockholders are going to get as much as the non-dissenting stockholders; the outcome can go either way.

Question: How would you value the shares of a company with 10 equal minority shareholders who have signed a buy-sell agreement at fair market value?

Pratt: One of the most troublesome things I have seen in my career has to do with this notion of buy-sell agreements and transactions among minority stockholders in closely held companies. This is a real problem when the individuals do not understand the concept of fair market value and what they are agreeing to in their methodology for setting prices.

If you write into the buy-sell agreement "fair market value of the subject shares" or something to that effect, it becomes quite apparent that the fair market value of these minority shares is going to be substantially less than a proportionate share of the enterprise value. People get into these agreements time after time with that kind of language, thinking that what that language means is a proportionate share of the enterprise value. If you are ever involved in drafting such agreements, please try to make sure that all of the parties understand the *implication* of the wording. The values can range from a proportionate share of the enterprise value to a strict fair market value. If the agreement is written "fair market value of these shares," appraisers are bound to value them as minority shares.

Fairness and Solvency Opinions

Chester A. Gougis

There is an inherent tension between fairness opinions and solvency opinions. Both involve an opinion on whether the value of securities or assets transferred in a proposed transaction is fair, but they have different purposes and are often performed for different parties.

The purpose of a fairness opinion is to advise a fiduciary on the value of a company that is involved in a transaction, typically the sale of an asset or the entire company. For example, a financial advisor might provide a board of directors with a fairness opinion on the value of a company that is being sold.

The purpose of a solvency opinion is to verify that a deal is solvent. Most solvency opinions are performed for the buyer side of a transaction. For example, a buyer will want an opinion on whether the price being paid is below the value of the asset being purchased.

All things equal, the provider of the fairness opinion to the seller is trying to ascertain whether the transaction price is *no less* than fair market value, and the provider of the solvency opinion to the buyer wants to assure that the price is *no greater* than the fair market value. As a result, it is rare that the person giving the fairness opinion and the person giving the solvency opinion can agree, unless the transaction happens to be done at the exact value representing the true economic value of the business.

Fairness Opinions

The main purpose of fairness opinions is to aid fiduciaries in making a decision that affects the people whose financial interests are at stake. These fiduciaries include boards of directors, Employee Stock Ownership Plan (ESOP) trustees, corporate debt trustees, bankruptcy trustees, and personal trustees.

Fairness opinions are financial opinions. They typically compare the estimated true economic value of an offer relative to the estimated true economic value of the company. If the transaction is an acquisition, the valuation may be on a control basis. If the transaction is a leveraged buyout, the valuation may be on a liquidation basis.

Fairness opinions do not address the interests of employees or creditors. They are directed toward one group—the shareholders of the company. As a result, the fairness opinion conclusion is based primarily on the valuation of the securities. Because it is a valuation opinion, it addresses the question, "Is the shareholder getting more than what he is paying for?" The question of whether the transaction is equitable is a separate issue. In some transactions, particularly LBOs, the selling shareholders may receive a considerable premium over the trading price—in some cases as much as a 100 percent premium. Key managers, however, through equity granted in the new company, may receive much more. Although this type of deal may not be equitable, it may be fair, which is what the fairness opinion is designed to measure.

Fairness opinions are becoming somewhat controversial. Part of the problem is that transactions are becoming more complex. In the past, most acquisitions involved one company buying another company, and the buyer and seller were clearly defined. Each side was represented by its own investment banker. In most cases, the investment banker had a long-standing relationship with the company and felt that one of its responsibilities was to give advice to the company and its board of directors about these types of transactions.

The financial environment has changed quite a bit in the past few years with the advent of leveraged buyouts, management buyouts, recapitalizations, and restructurings. Now, a company's investment banker may also be an equity participant in the proposed transaction—creating a conflict of interest. The calculation of fees creates another area of conflict of interest. In many cases, the size of the fee for a firm representing a company that has received a takeover offer depends on whether the offer is accepted. This creates a certain conflict of interest in terms of the pure advisory role these people play.

It is not just the external players who have conflicting roles, but also the internal players. Another area of potential conflict involves management's objectivity. In a takeover situation, management may sometimes be influenced by the desire to preserve the status quo—i.e., its own jobs. In other instances, management may be influenced by personal gains—such as a "golden parachute"—to support a takeover. Management may also play a key role as one of the bidders in a transaction. This is a cause for concern in transactions, because management may manipulate the process by using information about the company to which they have exclusive access.

As a result, a fairness opinion from an independent source is requested by the board of directors of a company when it is making a decision on a major transaction that will affect the shareholders of that company—for example, a merger, an acquisition, the sale of the entire company, a recapitalization or restructuring transaction, a management buyout, or a transaction involving some conflict of interest. The board of directors has a fiduciary responsibility to act in the best interest of the shareholders. Part of that responsibility, with respect to a major transaction, is obtaining outside advice from an expert as to whether the transaction is in the best interest of the shareholders.

Fairness opinions are also used by other fiduciaries who have the responsibility to protect another group's interests. Because of the nature of a fiduciary's responsibilities and liabilities, a fiduciary will always want an outside expert to confirm his or her own judgment. For example, fairness opinions are used to advise ESOP trustees on their responsibility in voting ESOP shares for or against transactions that affect the ESOP, which may have different interests than the shareholder group as a whole. Similarly, in situations of bankruptcy or restructuring where covenants have been violated or corporate debt trustees are asked to waive covenants, those trustees have a fiduciary responsibility to the bondholders to make sure that whatever action the company is taking benefits their particular constituency. Fairness opinions are also provided in some cases to personal trustees, who have a fiduciary responsibility to the beneficiaries of those trusts to make sure their actions are in the best interest of the beneficiaries.

Fairness opinions used to be almost solely the province of public companies. Because there was a diverse group of owners who had different interests, there was the possibility of class action suits. Also, because public companies were bigger—and the stakes were higher—it made more economic sense to get a fairness opinion. Increasingly, fairness opinions are being used in private companies. For one thing, private companies are getting bigger. In the past, when a company reached a certain size, it was almost inevitable that it went public. Now, there are a tremendous number of large private companies with no intention of going public. Often, as these companies grow and mature, the shareholders increase and become more diverse. The boards of directors of these larger private companies often include outside board members who recognize that they have a fiduciary responsibility to make sure the actions they are taking benefit all the shareholders rather than simply the members of a controlling family group. Also, there has been an increasing tendency for private-company situations to get "messy." That is, as the stakes get higher, once-cohesive family groups often break apart, accompanied by acrimonious litigation. As a result, there has been a trend toward private companies obtaining fairness opinions to validate some of the actions they are taking.

Legal and Regulatory Requirements of Fairness Opinions

Fairness opinions must comply with legal and regulatory requirements. With all the attention being paid to issues of fairness, it is surprising that there is no formal requirement for a company to get a fairness opinion. The decision is purely at the discretion of the board of directors of the company. If the board feels that it can determine whether an offer is fair, there is no requirement to obtain an outside opinion. The closest thing to a requirement is in private transactions where the company is buying some or all of the shares from the public—for example, a management buyout. Clearly, there would be a strong conflict of interest.

The Securities and Exchange Commission (SEC) requirements regarding fairness opinions deal mostly with disclosure. According to Rule 13e-3, directors must disclose the following factors: the current market price of the stock, the historical prices of the stock, the net book value of the stock, the going-concern value, the liquidation value, the price paid by the company in the past to repurchase its shares, outside fairness opinions or valuations, and other offers. Although the SEC does not require that a board get a fairness opinion, if one is received it must be disclosed.

Last year, U.S. Congressman Markey of Massachusetts introduced legislation requiring that a fairness opinion be obtained from an outside source—i.e., not the company's own investment bank—on any management buyout or similar transaction. The legislation was written to prevent "sweetheart" LBOs—deals where management came in with a quick offer to buy the company without entertaining other offers, and as a result bought the company at a very favorable price. It was argued that several deals in the early years of LBOs fell into this category. In recent years, as the visibility of these transactions to both regulators and alternative buyers increased, the ability of management to do this lessened. Many legislators still feel, however, that there is a need for regulation to address this particular issue.

Developments on the legal front have been the biggest impetus for directors to get fairness opinions. Although there is no law that creates an absolute requirement to get fairness opinions, several court decisions have held directors liable in takeover transactions in which it was determined that the directors did not act in the shareholders' best interest. These cases are somewhat extreme in the sense that the boards of directors clearly did not take the normal standard of care in representing shareholders. Nonetheless, it is pointed out that these directors do have a fiduciary responsibility to shareholders that must be taken very seriously.

Case law suggests that directors facing a takeover or buyout bid need to (1) establish a clear record of consideration of fairness, (2) obtain a fairness opinion, (3) ensure that the opinion is sufficiently thorough and extensive, (4) negotiate terms and price, and (5) seek other bidders in certain circumstances. Two cases establish the responsibility of independent directors in this area. One of these cases is Weinberger v. UOP, Inc., which was a "squeeze-out" merger; that is, a situation in which the corporate majority owner of a public company was causing a forced merger with the parent.[1] Interestingly, the directors had obtained a fairness opinion, but it was discovered to be a cursory opinion provided over the weekend by the company's own investment bank (which was also receiving significant fees in the transaction). In the other case, Smith v. Van Gorkem, the board did not get a fairness opinion.[2] It approved a fairly sizable acquisition only a few hours after hearing about it.

Directors can be held personally liable in some cases. This has been the principal motivation behind the increased focus on fairness opinions in takeover battles. Several court rulings in corporate takeover battles—for example, Revlon, SCM, and Freuhauf—suggest that at some point in a takeover transaction, directors may be required to conduct an auction. Fairness opinions may also need to address the fairness and adequacy of this auction process. Most lawyers indicate that directors must be able to demonstrate that they understand what is going on, even though a fairness opinion is not required by law. It helps to obtain a thorough review by a third party, including a fairness opinion.

[1]Weinberger v. UOP, Inc., 457 A.2d 701 (Del. Sup. Ct. 1983).

[2]Smith v. Van Gorkem, 488 A.2d 858 (Del. Sup. Ct. 1985).

Standards of Fairness

The standards of fairness depend on the definition of fair market value. The basis of valuation and the definition of fair market value depend on whether it is control value, minority-interest value, or a special buyer price, as well as other marketability considerations. The basis depends on the situation—for example, whether it is an acquisition of control, a squeeze-out merger, a recapitalization transaction, or an ESOP transaction.

It is important to distinguish between control value and minority-interest value in determining fairness. Are you measuring the going-concern value of a minority interest in the company, or are you estimating the value of 100 percent of the company sold to a third party? If a company was selling for $60 a share and then someone offers $80 a share, how can the board of directors turn down the offer that represents an easy $20-per-share profit? That offer might be very inadequate, however, if it is for a controlling interest in the company. Perhaps the company would be worth $90 or $100 per share if the board auctioned it off.

In private companies, this issue is further exacerbated by the fact that a minority interest in a private company is nonmarketable. In fact, it can be argued that it is worth almost nothing if the company does not pay any dividends. Controlling interests in private companies, however, are often sold at prices that represent a multiple of earnings similar to the multiples paid for public companies. Therefore, the basis of valuation—control versus minority—is even more critical to private-company fairness opinions.

Clearly, then, the definition of fair market value and the resulting determination of fairness depend on the situation. In cases involving the acquisition of a controlling interest, the usual standard is control value. The most common valuation technique used to measure control value is discounted-cash-flow analysis. Prices paid in comparable acquisition transactions are also used. Break-up values and an understanding of any synergistic benefits should also be considered in a control valuation. This is particularly important in LBO transactions, where the buyers are often financial buyers. One of the standards used to determine whether this kind of deal is fair is to ask what the value would be if the deal were thrown open to nonfinancial buyers, and they were given a fair shot at buying the company. In many cases, nonfinancial buyers are able to benefit from synergies that financial buyers would not be able to obtain, thereby raising the value of the firm.

In squeeze-out mergers, where the majority owner is forcing a minority holder to sell out, the standards are not as clear. Buyers usually offer a premium above minority-interest value in these transactions, but the premium is not as high as the premium for a 100-percent-buyout transaction. The decision between using the going-concern value or a control value depends in part on the state in which the target is incorporated and the rights accorded the minority holders by the laws of that state.

In recapitalization transactions, the key factor is whether the controlling interest has changed. The main question concerns the rights minority shareholders have if they do not accept the recapitalization offer. In such transactions, the public shareholders are usually left with stub securities. In the RJR deal, for example, the shareholders received some securities. The exact value of those securities is probably the most critical element in determining whether those transactions are fair.

In ESOP transactions, there is some controversy over the amount of the ESOP's investment (because the ESOP pays). Recent regulations indicate that control value is appropriate only when ESOP owns more than 50 percent of the equity, regardless of whether the ESOP is part of a control group. There are also Department of Labor regulations that further complicate matters.

Due-Diligence Requirements

There are several standard due-diligence requirements in fairness opinions. These include company and plant visits and reviews of historical information, management projections, and other public industry information. Additional steps are required in some transactions: Boards may be required to solicit other bids in management buyouts, trustees may be required to negotiate actively on ESOP transactions, and everyone may be required to scrutinize company-provided information in situations where management has a conflict of interest.

Solvency Opinions

Solvency opinions are very different from fairness opinions because they are typically for the benefit of the secured lenders, corporate directors, and selling shareholders who face the risk of claims of fraudulent conveyance in highly leveraged transactions. A solvency opinion can lessen the risk of fraudulent conveyance if it represents a good-faith effort to determine solvency. The courts have denied claims of fraudulent conveyance when the original credit

decision was based on reasonable analyses.[3]

The concept of fraudulent-conveyance risk originates from a legal doctrine dating from sixteenth-century English Common Law. More modern definitions of the concept are found in the Uniform Fraudulent Conveyance Act and the Bankruptcy Code in the United States. A fraudulent conveyance is defined as any transfer which (1) is made with the actual intent to hinder, delay, or defraud an existing creditor; (2) is made for inadequate consideration by an undercapitalized business; and (3) is made for inadequate consideration by one intending to incur debts beyond one's ability to pay as they mature. For example, one cannot do a leveraged buyout of a company worth only $100 million for $120 million by letting the senior banks take security against the original assets of $90-95 million. In essence, they have received all of the value, and there is hardly any value left for unsecured creditors. If the company declares bankruptcy shortly thereafter, the banks have security on all these assets, but the unsecured creditors have nothing because all the assets of the company which they thought were supporting their everyday credit are gone.

In the Resorts International deal involving Merv Griffin and Donald Trump, the unsecured creditors are suing Griffin and Trump on the basis of fraudulent conveyance. They claim that Griffin paid too much for the company and that the banks were willing to loan into this deal because they received all the assets as security. In any restructuring, the people who will get hurt are the unsecured creditors.

Three elements are addressed in most solvency opinions. First, there is a balance-sheet test, which attempts to determine whether the company's assets are worth more than the liabilities it is taking on. Second, there is a cash-flow test, which attempts to determine whether the company will be able to generate enough of a cash flow to meet its obligations. Finally, there is a capital-adequacy test, which attempts to determine whether the company has enough capital for the businesses in which it is engaged.

The definition of key terms is important in solvency opinions. "Fair value" is defined in terms of the going-concern value of the company rather than the value of the individual assets. It also involves consideration of the impact of the costs of a sale, valuation techniques, and the assumed timing of the sale. The definition of "liabilities" is also important. It is generally interpreted to denote the face value of the debt rather than the market value of the debt.

[3]See, for example, Credit Managers Association v. Federal Company, 629 F. Supp. 175 (C.D. Cal. 1986).

Also, contingent liabilities and the probability of their occurrence must be included. Finally, subsidiary guarantees must be included to the extent it is likely that they will be relied upon.

The bottom line on solvency opinions is that they are even more difficult to give than fairness opinions because one is not only making some assumptions about value—i.e., that the value of the assets are greater than the liabilities—but also about the company's ongoing ability to meet its debt obligations. Solvency opinions involve both a valuation and a credit analysis.

Question and Answer Session

Question: Do you think the firm that puts a deal together should also write the fairness opinion?

Gougis: No, I do not think that is appropriate, but I have a biased opinion because we clearly represent ourselves as being independent when we do this work. In many firms, there is a conflict of interest. If an investment banker puts a deal together, the firm can sometimes earn fees of $10 to $20 million. The charge for a fairness opinion is typically $300,000 to $500,000. Thus, if the investment banker says no in the fairness opinion, the firm earns considerably less than if it says yes and then puts the deal together.

Pratt: This is a very controversial subject. There is a trend away from the dealmaker also providing a fairness opinion. In fact, in the case of ESOPs, it is absolutely taboo: Nobody can take a fee for putting the ESOP deal together and also doing the fairness opinion.

Gougis: From a practical point of view, it is not done in management buyouts, either, because of the recognition that frequently the investment banker putting the deal together is also investing in the deal with management.

Question: Is there a systematic difference in either the values or the techniques applied between investment bankers doing valuation or fairness work and financial advisors with no banking relationships?

Gougis: There are fewer differences in the techniques used now compared with 10 years ago, when an investment banker's opinion did not generally incorporate discounted-cash-flow models. That has really changed. There is a difference, however, in the emphasis placed on intuitive feeling (investment bankers) versus hard analysis (valuation firms).

Preferred Stocks, Bonds, and Specialized Securities

Marko A. Budgyk

Most of the presentations in these proceedings focus on issues that impact the residual value of the common stock of a corporation. This presentation, however, provides an overview of the other securities that make up a company's capital structure, particularly bonds and preferred stocks.

Bonds and Preferred Stocks

In many ways, the valuation of fixed-income securities is both similar to and different from the valuation of equity securities. For example, the typical valuation method for bonds and preferred stocks is the discounted-cash-flow approach. The value of any security is a function of two basic components: a future income stream, and a discount rate that reflects the uncertainty of realizing that stream. Although the valuation of all securities is similar to some extent, the differences between bonds, preferred stocks, and equities require some modifications to the valuation methods. Because the future cash flows expected from fixed-income securities are contractually specified, the primary valuation task is to select an appropriate discount rate.

The major difference between equity securities and most fixed-income securities—e.g., nonconvertible fixed-income securities and preferred stocks—is that the income stream is contractually predetermined and usually of finite duration for the fixed-income securities. Because most fixed-income securities have a maturity, one does not have to estimate a residual value. Also, because the income stream is contractually predetermined, there is very little uncertainty about the cash flows. If the security does not default, the magnitude of the cash flows is known with certainty. If the security does default, the remaining cash flows are zero. Thus, there are fewer possible scenarios for fixed-income securities: Either everything is paid according to the contract, or it is not. When things do not work out, there are several possible outcomes, but much of the uncertainty in the valuation has been reduced because analysts need not forecast growth rates. Because the only area of uncertainty is associated with default,

the probability of default must be considered in the valuation methodology of fixed-income securities.

The differences between preferred stocks and nonconvertible bonds are shown in **Table 1**. The main differences are their relative priority of claim on the assets and income of the issuing firm, the tax treatment to the issuer, the tax treatment to the holder, the consequences of missed payments, and the duration of the security. Both types of securities participate *indirectly* in the firm's growth. As companies improve their financial positions, their operating performance improves, which causes the riskiness of these securities to decrease. As the risk decreases, the prices increase. So, there is a high correlation between the value of common stock and the value of preferred stocks and debt: As a firm grows and becomes less risky, the value of its bonds and its preferred stocks will also increase.

The tax treatment to investors is different because bondholders must recognize interest income as ordinary income, whereas corporations owning preferred stock may exclude 80 percent of preferred dividends from their income. Empirical studies indicate that preferred stocks trade at prices that reflect this tax exclusion—e.g., the buy-and-sell activity of corporate security holders establishes the yield on preferred stocks at relatively low levels by bidding the prices up, because they experience significant tax advantages from ownership. Because corporations wish to retain the option of changing their capital structures, most preferred securities contain a provision that permits their early retirement, typically a call feature or a redemption provision.

Various characteristics of securities influence their relative yield and, thus, their value. Two key factors that affect the relative yields of bonds versus preferred stocks are the relative claim on the issuing firm's income and assets and the differential tax treatment. These factors work in opposite directions. The fact that bonds are senior to preferred stocks in the capital structure suggests that they are less risky and therefore have lower yields than preferred stocks. On the other hand, the different tax treatment of holders of these securities suggests that lower yields are acceptable for preferred stocks relative to bonds. Which force is greater? Empirical work has shown that for very good investment-grade issuers, the tax-exclusion effect dominates, and preferred-stock yields are lower than bond yields. When the issuing company is a high-risk firm, the position of the claim on income and assets tends to dominate, and bond yields are lower than preferred-stock yields.

Determination of the Discount Rate

Discount rates are an important part of the fixed-income-security valuation process. There are two basic determinants of discount rates for fixed-income securities: company-specific risk and issue-specific risk. In practice, the two cannot be completely divorced.

Company-specific risk is the portion of risk based on the credit quality of the company. Company-specific risk refers to the probability of default or missed dividends. It contains two components: *financial risk* and *operating risk*. Financial risk is a function of a firm's capital structure, measured in terms of the relative proportions of debt and equity. Operating risk is the degree of uncertainty surrounding a firm's future operating performance.

Financial risk is fairly easy to measure. It is a function of the nature of a firm's capital structure and the obligation placed upon the cash flows of a company. To measure the degree of financial risk, it is important to classify securities as debt or equity based on their economic characteristics, rather than on how they have been classified in the financial statements.

The two features that characterize debt are that the cash flows are contractually fixed, and nonpayment can force bankruptcy. The term "contractually fixed" does not exclude securities with floating rates; rather, it means that those rates are set by a contract. Equity, on the other hand, is characterized by cash flows that are residual, contingent, and variable, and nonpayment cannot force bankruptcy. It is important to understand this distinction because there are securities that possess elements of both debt and equity. The financial risk of a company is related to how much debt *risk* is being placed upon the company, rather than just how much debt exists. Some examples of securities with both debt and equity properties are redeemable preferred, convertible preferred, and convertible debt. Leverage ratios are a good way of measuring the relative financial risk. Three possible ratios are debt to equity, preferred to common, and cash flow to fixed charges.

Operating risk is a little harder to measure than financial risk. It is the degree of uncertainty surrounding a firm's future operating performance. For financial risk, there are only a few ways to measure the leverage in a firm's capital structure. There are several corporate characteristics associated with operating risk: cost structure, product obsolescence, the necessity of product, the frequency of purchase of product, cyclicality of demand, and susceptibility to raw material prices. High fixed costs tend to imply high operating risk. Similarly, rapid obsolescence implies—more often than not—high operating risk. Operating risk is reduced when the product is a necessary item and is purchased frequently. Of

---

TABLE 1. Nonconvertible Bonds Versus Preferred Stocks

	Bonds	*Preferred Stocks*
Position in capital structure	Senior to preferred	Junior to debt
Tax treatment of interest/ dividends to issuer	Tax deductible	Not tax deductible
Tax treatment of interest/ dividends to holder	Regular income	80% excluded from corporate income tax
Consequence of missed payments	Default: Can creditors force bankruptcy?	Accumulate as arrearages—cannot force bankruptcy
Participation in firm's growth	Indirect	Indirect

Source: Houlihan, Lokey, Howard & Zukin, Inc.

course, high cyclicality of demand and a high susceptibility to raw-material price changes also imply high operating risk. Automobile manufacturers and steel companies are examples of companies with high operating risk; grocery stores and utilities are examples of low-operating-risk companies.

There are two relatively good measures of operating risk. The first is stock-price volatility. Volatility is a measure of the tendency to change, and people who own fixed-income securities typically do not want a company's circumstances to change. As a reference point, it would be valuable to estimate the stock-price volatility of the company being valued by an analysis of the volatility of other companies in the same line of business. Another means of measuring operating risk is the historical variance of operating performance. This may be in terms of the variance of revenues, operating income, or cash flow. The historical comparison shows how things have changed from year to year: Large year-to-year changes indicate substantial operating risk; small changes indicate little operating risk.

Issue-specific risk is the portion of risk of a security emanating from contractual rights and specifications of the individual issue. Every fixed-income security has a contract that specifies the options of the holder if the company does not meet its contractual obligations versus the options that the company has. Different combinations of these rights and privileges imply different amounts of issue-specific risk.

There are myriad variations of issue-specific risk. Most of them can be categorized into the following five groups: dividend/interest protection, asset protection or liquidation preference, refinancing risk or callability, voting rights, and transferability. Some types of clauses protect the issuer; others, the holder.

The first category is dividend or interest protection. Priority of claim to the cash flows of the firm is one of the rights built into every fixed-income security. Bonds have a prior claim to the cash flows of the issuing firm (relative to equity securities). Preferred stocks have priority over common stocks but are subordinate to bonds. In determining the degree of priority of preferred stock over common stock, one should determine whether the preferred dividend is cumulative. There are many closely held non-cumulative preferreds out there, but very few publics. Obviously, this affects the way the preferred will be valued, particularly if the preferred has skipped a dividend. It will probably also have a discount for lack of marketability because it has no rights to compel dividends.

Bonds are always cumulative if they are current-

pay instruments, but special features, such as resetable rates and floating rates, have been added to some issues to protect bondholders. A floating rate is tied to a specific mechanism; a resetable rate is one that basically guarantees the holder a return to par. For a bondholder, a resetable rate is better because it protects against changes in credit quality as well as interest rates, whereas a floating rate only protects against changes in interest rates.

The second category of issue-specific risk is asset protection or liquidation priority. As with dividends and interest, bonds have a liquidation priority over all equity, and preferred stocks have a liquidation priority over common stocks. The value of this feature depends on the alternative value of the assets and the size of the claims against those assets. Preferred shareholders are not in a strong position in the event of liquidation.

The third category is refinancing risk or callability. A call option gives a corporation the right to buy its bonds or preferred stock back if interest rates become more attractive (decline). This has the effect of shortening the maturity of a bond issue, which can adversely affect investors. Call options can also hurt investors because they can limit price appreciation.

Voting rights are another category, but not a very important one in terms of the value of fixed-income securities. Quite simply, they do not exist for bonds, and although some preferred issues have voting rights, typically there are not enough votes in a class of preferred to affect corporate policy. Voting rights mean far more in the valuation of common stock.

The last category is transferability rights. Nonmarketable preferreds are worth less than similar marketable preferreds, but the discount tends to be smaller for the common stock because part of the return is in dividends, which are always marketable when paid in cash.

The Valuation Process

The valuation process for fixed-income securities of closely held companies is very similar to that for common stocks of closely held companies. The first step in valuing the debt is to look for public comparables. In the selection of comparables, emphasis should be placed on securities that have similarities in capital features, other issue-specific features, and lines of business. In considering the value of a subordinated issue, the comparables should be subordinated issues. Likewise, other issue-specific features should be matched; for example, nonconvertibles with nonconvertibles, floating-rate issues with floating-rate issues, and so forth. A similar line of business is not as important for fixed-income securities because growth is not as important. The discount rate is chosen by determining the yields on comparable issues and making the appropriate adjustments for differences in financial risk, operating risk, and issue-specific risk.

Valuation of Convertible Securities

The favored valuation approach for convertible fixed-income securities of closely held companies is a version of the discounted-cash-flow approach. Some people value convertibles as a combination of an option and straight debt, but we favor an approach that considers the value of a convertible to be the combination of a common stock and a nonconvertible preferred or debt security. The components of value, therefore, are twofold: the conversion value (the common-stock equivalent) and the present value of excess dividends or interest. The conversion value equals the value of common stock into which the security may be immediately converted—i.e., its conversion rate times the price per common share. It may be thought of as a security's terminal value, because convertibles are generally issued with the intent of ultimate conversion.

Excess dividends or interest form the other portion of the convertible's value. Convertibles trade at a premium above convertible value, typically 10 to 50 percent higher. The reason for the premium is that the current return on a convertible is greater than the return one would get by converting into the common. Two factors will affect the premium: the trend of dividends on the common stock, and the time until the conversion is either forced or accomplished voluntarily. These factors must be considered in determining what this premium is worth. As the dividend on the common stock increases, the premium of the convertible preferred or convertible debt will go down because the difference between the convertible yield and the dividend yield on the common stock has decreased. Another factor affecting the premium is the uncertainty about how long these extra dividends on the convertible will be received. This will depend upon the growth rate of the dividends on the common stock. Typically, convertible securities listed on the New York Stock Exchange sell at a premium of three to four years of the current extra dividends.

Question and Answer Session

Question: How do changes in the level of interest rates affect the valuation of fixed-income securities?

Budgyk: Most fixed-income securities are very sensitive to the level of interest rates. In general, higher rates reduce value, whereas lower rates increase value. The degree to which value changes in response to interest-rate changes is referred to as duration. The more distant in time a bond's cash flow, the greater its duration and the greater its sensitivity to interest rates.

Question: How do expectations about inflation affect the valuation of fixed-income securities?

Budgyk: Expectations about inflation are typically reflected in interest rates. Expectations of higher rates, for example, would translate into lower valuations.

Question: In your presentation, you listed stock-price volatility as a good measure of operating risk. How can stock-price volatility be calculated for a closely held company or an inactively traded security?

Budgyk: One can estimate volatility or operating risk for a closely-held company through analysis of a group of comparables.

Question: What contractual covenants in a fixed-income security provide the most protection in the event of bankruptcy?

Budgyk: In a bankruptcy, the best covenant is to have a secured and prior interest in a pledged asset or group of assets.

The Appraisal Report: Current Standards, Proper Format, and Common Errors

Frank C. Carr, Jr.

Once an appraisal of the value of a firm is complete, a report must be written. The presentation of the appraisal report is important for two reasons. First, the appraisal report is the only tangible evidence the client receives when he hires a valuation consultant. The client deserves to know, and in many cases *must* know, how the conclusions were reached and what assumptions and judgments were employed to arrive at them. Furthermore, the quality of the report strongly influences the client's thinking as to the quality of the valuation consultant.

Second, judges rely on appraisal reports when they write their opinions. Judges are beginning to handle valuation opinions differently than they have in the past. They are no longer merely interested in splitting the difference between the valuations, nor are they willing to accept an expert's statements without alteration. In fact, judges are beginning to view an expert opinion as just another opinion, and like any other judgments, those of an expert can be no better than the soundness of the reasons that support them. Appraisers must document their conclusions. An appraiser may have the world's most accurate conclusion, but if he or she cannot demonstrate to a third party that the conclusion is correct, it is not worth much.

The Appraisal Report

The appraisal report represents an opportunity for clients to appraise the appraiser. Appraisers should use the report to present the facts and circumstances that dictated what they did, the assumptions they made, and how the conclusions were reached. An appraiser probably will not satisfy his client unless the entire report is built on a foundation that includes these aspects.

Appraisal reports are used for several purposes. The major uses include potential sale, potential purchase, litigation, tax purposes, trustee allocation (ESOP), marital property settlement, credit analysis, corporate planning, and public offerings. The prem-

ise of value and the value itself will probably change with each purpose. Only the report can indicate this. In most cases, the end users of these reports will not know very much about valuation, so the appraiser must educate them.

The appraisal report is the only tangible evidence the client receives as a result of a rather costly process of obtaining an appraisal. That tangible evidence must be valid over a period of time—not only when it is written, but also in the future if litigation occurs. In addition, the report must be able to stand alone as a resource for the primary users as well as for third-party users. As specified in their Code of Ethics, members of the American Society of Appraisers (ASA) have a fiduciary responsibility to third-party users.

The Standards

The Principles of Appraisal Practice and Code of Ethics of the ASA set forth standards for appraisal reports. Section 8 presents the minimum required standards. Listed in this section are such fundamental items as

1. the parts of an appraisal report;
2. how to describe the property that is the subject of the appraisal report;
3. a statement of the objectives of the appraisal work, including the premise of value, the date, and the purpose;
4. a statement of the contingent and limiting conditions to which the appraisal findings are subject, including sources of data, limiting factors, and whether the valuation is hypothetical, fractional, or preliminary;
5. a description and explanation in the appraisal report of the appraisal method(s) used;
6. a statement of the appraiser's disinterestedness;
7. information about the signatures on the appraisal report; and

8. the inclusion of dissenting opinions.

Signatures are a controversial topic now. The ASA standard states that all of the people who prepared the report must be identified. Firms that provide a corporate signature should conform to this standard.

The standard also states that appraisals must conform to a set of standards formulated by federal legislation—the Uniform Standards of Professional Appraisal Practice (USPAP)—which is the responsibility of The Appraisal Foundation. States are using this legislation as the model when they adopt valuation certification and licensing standards.

Standard 10 of USPAP addresses appraisal reporting. This standard stresses that an appraiser must communicate each analysis, opinion, and conclusion in a manner that is not misleading. This applies to both written and oral business reports. The key sections of Standard 10 are outlined below.

Standard 10-1. Each written or oral business appraisal report must

1. clearly and accurately set forth the appraisal in a manner that will not be misleading;
2. contain sufficient information to enable the person(s) who receives or relies on the report to understand it properly; and
3. clearly and accurately disclose any extraordinary assumptions or limiting conditions that directly affect the appraisal, and indicate their impact on value.

Standard 10-2. Each written business appraisal report must comply with the following specific reporting guidelines:

1. identify and describe the business enterprise, asset, or equity being appraised;
2. state the purpose of the appraisal;
3. define the value to be estimated;
4. set forth the effective date of the appraisal and the date of the report;
5. describe the scope of the appraisal;
6. set forth all assumptions and limiting conditions that affect the analyses, opinions, and conclusions;
7. set forth the information considered, the appraisal procedures followed, and the reasoning that supports the analyses, opinions, and conclusions;
8. set forth any additional information that may be appropriate to show compliance with, or clearly identify and explain permitted departures from, the requirements of Standard 9 (which outlines the considerations in writing a valuation report); and

9. include a certification in accordance with Standard 10-3.

Standard 10-3. Each written business appraisal report must contain a certification that is similar in content to the following:

I certify that, to the best of my knowledge and belief:

- The statements of fact contained in this report are true and correct.
- The reported analyses, opinions, and conclusions are limited only by the reported assumptions and limiting conditions, and are my personal, unbiased professional analyses, opinions, and conclusions.
- I have no [or the specified] present or prospective interest in the property that is the subject of this report, and I have no [or the specified] personal interest or bias with respect to the parties involved.
- My compensation is not contingent on an action or event resulting from the analyses, opinions, or conclusions in, or the use of, this report.
- My analyses, opinions, and conclusions were developed, and this report has been prepared, in conformity with the Uniform Standards of Professional Appraisal Practice.
- No one provided significant professional assistance to the person signing this report. [If there are exceptions, the name of each individual providing significant professional assistance must be stated.]

Standard 10-4. To the extent that it is possible *and* appropriate, each oral business appraisal report (including expert testimony) must address the substantive matters (reporting guidelines) set forth in Standard 10-2, described earlier.

Standard 10-5. An appraiser who signs a business appraisal report prepared by another, even under the label "review appraiser," must accept full responsibility for the contents of the report.

Typical Report Format

The typical appraisal report comprises a transmittal letter, an introduction, a description of the economy, a description of the industry, a statement on the fundamental position of the company, a financial statement analysis, a description of the valuation methods used, a discussion of contingent and limiting conditions, an appraiser's certification, and appendixes presenting any backup data.

The length of the report depends on the facts and circumstances of the situation and what the client needs. There are many required elements in an appraisal report. If a section is omitted, there must be a good reason for omitting it.

Transmittal letter. A transmittal letter describing some of the salient features of what was done typically accompanies the appraisal report. In many cases, the transmittal letter contains the valuation conclusion and signatures. This letter can often satisfy some of the client's needs from a reporting perspective.

Introduction. Typically, an introduction describes the assignment, contains a summary description of the company, a definition of the premise of value, the sources of information, a summary, and a conclusion. The description of the assignment should include an exact description of the property under appraisal, the date of the appraisal, the purpose of the appraisal, and the client.

Valuation premises. It is important to define the valuation premises being used and to get the client's agreement that they are the appropriate conditions, rather than to make assumptions. Frequently, the premise will be fair market value. Definitions of fair market value are contained in Revenue Ruling 59-60, Revenue Ruling 83-120, and other sources.

Background of the company. The report must contain basic information about the company. This includes general background information on the economy, the industry in which the company operates, and the fundamental position of the company within the industry. It also includes specific information such as a financial statement analysis, a trend analysis, a comparative industry analysis, the outlook for the industry, and the outlook for the company.

Valuation procedures. The report must contain a description of valuation approaches, an analysis of similar publicly traded companies, comments on any adjustments made to the balance sheet or income statement, an estimate of current earning power, and a projection of the cash flows if a discounted-cash-flow analysis is being used. In many cases, the report will contain descriptions of valuation approaches that were considered but discarded and the reasons those approaches could not be used. **Exhibit 1** lists alternative valuation approaches.

Reconciliation. The appraisal section must include a reconciliation of the valuations obtained using different approaches. The reconciliation must lead to a conclusion. An appraiser must weigh each of the approaches used in terms of its validity as an indication of value in the current situation.

Report appendixes. Appendixes to a report will generally fall within three categories:

1. a statement of the contingent and limiting conditions to which the appraisal findings

are subject;

2. an appraiser's certification in conformity with Standard 10-3 of the USPAP; and

3. procedural or informational exhibits that amplify or back up data or statements made in the body of the report.

Errors, Omissions, and Shortcomings

Appraisal reports may contain two general types of errors: (1) valuation errors, or (2) presentation errors or omissions. Analysis of several hundred reports submitted to the American Society of Appraisers indicates several common valuation errors. A listing of the most common errors is presented in **Exhibit 2**. It is significant that the most common error in this category is the failure to properly select, define, or conform to the standard of value appropriate to the valuation purpose. An error of this sort practically insures that all of the valuation work that follows will lead to a conclusion inappropriate to the client's needs, no matter how well crafted. The remaining valuation errors should be used as a checklist for any analyst reviewing the work, whether the valuation has reached the report stage or not.

The presentation errors or omissions set forth in **Exhibit 3** come from the same study. It is important to remember that a valuation assignment may be technically well done, but if it is not presented correctly, there is no way for someone to understand or appreciate it. Inadequate documentation is the major source of presentation error. The second most common problem is incoherence—a general failure to explain what was done in such a way that a reader may follow and verify the conclusion.

Other problems consist of a variety of omissions, imbalances of material presented, the use of confusing jargon, and poor or missing descriptions of what was done.

Conclusion

The preparation of an appraisal report is frequently the consultant's least favorite task. To the client and other readers, however, the report is very influential in forming their opinions about the consultant and the firm. Therefore, the report must be considered an integral step in the valuation process and be given the appropriate amount of attention. Properly prepared, the report can provide tangible evidence of professionalism. A poorly prepared report may lead to misuse, misunderstandings, and potential litigation.

EXHIBIT 1. Valuation Approaches

1. Price/Earnings Approach—Publicly Traded
2. Price/Book Approach—Publicly Traded
3. Price/Sales Approach—Publicly Traded
4. Price/Dividend Approach—Publicly Traded
5. Search for Similar Companies That Have Been Acquired
6. Price/Earnings Approach—Acquisitions
7. Price/Sales Approach—Acquisitions
8. Price/Book Approach—Acquisitions
9. Tangible Assets Plus Intangible Assets Approach
10. Capitalization of Earning Power Approach
11. Capitalization of Cash Flow Approach
12. Present Value of Future Earnings Approach
13. Discounted Cash Flow Approach
14. Investment Approach
15. Dividend Paying Capacity Approach
16. Seller's Discretionary Cash Approach
17. Market Data Approach

EXHIBIT 2. Valuation Errors

1. Failure to properly select, define, or conform to the standard of value appropriate to the valuation purpose
2. Internal inconsistencies
3. Comparative data problems
   a. Use of inappropriate public comparables
   b. Failure to adjust comparative company financial results
4. Undocumented or ungrounded variables
5. Computational errors
6. Misuse of subject company historical financial statements (failure to adjust or re-state)
7. Financial statement analysis errors
8. Application of earnings multiples to inappropriate earnings streams
9. Discounted-cash-flow errors
10. Rate-of-return selection errors
11. Application of rates of return to inappropriate earnings streams
12. Timing problems (application of multiples or rates of return from one period to earnings from a different period)
13. Failure to consider liquidity or control questions
14. Reliance on undocumented "rules of thumb"

EXHIBIT 3. Presentation Errors

1. Inadequate documentation
2. Incoherence (general failure to explain the valuation process, assumptions, etc. such that a reader can follow and verify the conclusion)
3. Failure to set forth or define the appropriate standard of value
4. Failure to set forth the purpose of the appraisal
5. Failure to set forth the date of the appraisal
6. Failure to set forth the limiting conditions
7. Presentational imbalance
8. Irrelevant information
9. Undefined jargon
10. Inadequate description of methodology
11. No statement of disinterestedness
12. Improper signature

Question and Answer Session

Question: Should an appraiser use more than one valuation approach in an appraisal?

Carr: Absolutely. The greater the number of valuation approaches that are presented, the better the report—within reason, of course. It is better to present several approaches that fit together logically than to present eight or ten different approaches that seem to be more of an exposition as to the appraiser's ability to employ different approaches than an attempt to arrive at an accurate value. If several approaches are presented, be sure to draw a conclusion as to the value.

Question: Are key-person discounts allowed when the key man is still alive?

Pratt: Yes, particularly in smaller companies. A smaller company is worth more to the extent that the key person is willing to stay with that company and assist materially in the transition than if the key person sells the company and disappears.

Reference List

Bishop, J.A. and I.A. Howitt. 1989. *Federal Tax Valuation Digest.* Cumulative edition. Boston: Warren, Gorham & Lamont.

Coolidge, H.C. 1975. "Fixing the Value of Minority Interest in a Business: Actual Sales Suggest as High as Seventy Percent." *Estate Planning* (Spring): 141.

——————. 1983. "Survey Shows Trend Toward Larger Minority Discounts." *Estate Planning* (September): 282.

Emory, J.D. 1985. "The Value of Marketability as Illustrated in Initial Public Offerings of Common Stock— January 1980 Through June 1981." *Business Valuation News* (September): 21-24.

——————. 1986. "The Value of Marketability as Illustrated in Initial Public Offerings of Common Stock—January 1985 Through June 1986." *Business Valuation Review* (December): 12-14.

Fellows, M.L. and W.H. Painter. 1978. "Valuing Close Corporations for Federal Wealth Transfer Taxes: A Statutory Solution to the Disappearing Wealth Syndrome." *Stanford Law Review* 30 (May): 909.

Gelman, M. 1972. "An Economist-Financial Analyst's Approach to Valuing Stock of a Closely Held Company." *Journal of Taxation* (June): 353-54.

Houlihan, Lokey, Howard & Zukin, Inc. 1989. *Control Premium Study.* Los Angeles.

Ibbotson, R.G. and R.A. Sinquefield. 1989. *Stocks, Bonds, Bills and Inflation: Historical Returns (1926-1987).* Charlottesville, VA: The Research Foundation of the Institute of Chartered Financial Analysts. (Data updated annually by Ibbotson Associates, Inc.)

Maher, J.M. 1976. "Discounts for Lack of Marketability for Closely Held Business Interests." *Taxes* (September): 562-71.

Moroney, R.E. 1973. "Most Courts Overvalue Closely Held Stocks." *Taxes* (March): 144-54.

Porter, M.E. 1980. *Competitive Strategy.* New York: The Free Press.

Pratt, S.P. 1986. *Valuing Small Businesses and Professional Practices.* Homewood, IL: Dow Jones-Irwin.

——————. 1989. *Valuing a Business: The Analysis and Appraisal of Closely Held Companies,* Second Edition. Homewood, IL: Dow Jones-Irwin.

Trout, R.R. 1977. "Estimation of the Discount Associated with the Transfer of Restricted Securities." *Taxes* (June): 381-85.

"Revenue Ruling 77-287 Revisited." 1983. *SRC Quarterly Reports* (Spring): 1-3.

U.S. Congress. House. 1971. "Discounts Involved in Purchases of Common Stock (1966-1969)." *Institutional Investor Study Report of the Securities and Exchange Commission.* H.R. Doc. No. 64, Part 5, 92d Cong., 1st Sess., pp. 2444-56.

Self-Evaluation Examination

1. Identify the correct statement about Revenue Ruling 59-60.
    a. It prevents the use of the discounted-cash-flow approach in estate- and gift-tax cases.
    b. It is considered to be too general to provide useful guidance in valuing closely held companies.
    c. It applies to closely held stock valuations as well as estate- and gift-tax valuations.
    d. It prevents the use of the market approach in estate- and gift-tax cases.

2. The term "fair value":
    a. Is synonymous with "fair market value."
    b. Is synonymous with "liquidation value."
    c. Is the price at which property would change hands between a willing buyer and a willing seller, when neither is under compulsion to enter the transaction, and both have a reasonable knowledge of relevant facts.
    d. Is the value minority stockholders should receive in a merger that is approved by the majority shareholders.

3. The value of shares held in a voting trust:
    a. Should be valued at a discount.
    b. Should be valued at a premium.
    c. Should not be adjusted either up or down solely because they are held in a voting trust.
    d. Should sometimes be discounted and sometimes be valued at a premium.

4. When selecting and evaluating publicly traded companies that are comparable to the firm being valued (using the market-value approach) it is important to do all of the following *except*:
    a. Delete firms having more than one line of business.
    b. Consider differences in the growth rates of sales, assets, and profitability.
    c. Recognize and adjust for differences in fiscal years.
    d. Perform a common-size analysis.

5. When comparing the financial statements of comparable companies as part of the market-value approach to valuation:
    a. The statements should all be adjusted to reflect the use of FIFO inventory accounting.
    b. The statements should all be adjusted to reflect the use of LIFO inventory accounting.
    c. The materiality of FIFO reserves should be considered.
    d. The materiality of LIFO reserves should be considered.

6. Making adjustments in the financial statements of closely held companies to reflect the impact of owners' and officers' compensation, as well as for the existence of significant non-operating assets, is important when using the market-value approach to valuation and _____ interest is at issue.
    a. Minority.
    b. Controlling.
    c. Both a and b.
    d. Neither a nor b.

7. Which of the following alternatives is most likely to be used when valuing a firm using the market-value approach?
    a. The price-to-cash-flow ratio and cash flow over the most recent six months.
    b. The price-to-cost-of-goods-sold (CGS) ratio and CGS over the most recent six months.
    c. The price-to-cash-flow ratio and cash flow over the most recent 12 months.
    d. The price-to-cost-of-goods-sold (CGS) ratio and CGS over the most recent 12 months.

8. Free cash flow can be defined as net income, plus depreciation and amortization: (i) less increases in working capital; (ii) less debt principal repayments; (iii) less interest on long-term debt; or (iv) less capital expenditures.
   a. i and iv.
   b. ii and iii.
   c. i, ii, and iv.
   d. ii, iii, and iv.

9. Which of the following is not a common adjustment made to net income to estimate the level of *recurring* cash flows?
   a. Deduct income and expense related to non-operating assets.
   b. Adjust owner compensation to reflect market-level compensation.
   c. Adjust actual lease rates to reflect economic lease rates.
   d. Add back to net income the compensation of all relatives of the owner.

10. When using the following equation to determine the terminal value of a firm as part of the discounted-cash-flow approach to valuation, which of the following assumptions is necessary?

$$value \ = \ \frac{CF_1}{i-g}$$

   a. The cash flows grow at a constant rate to infinity.
   b. The growth rate must exceed investor-required rates of return.
   c. The discount rate does not reflect future inflation.
   d. The growth rate must exceed zero.

11. When estimating the risk-free rate to use in the discounted-cash-flow method of valuation, a severely inverted yield curve would suggest using the yield on:
   a. 30-day Treasury bills.
   b. 180-day Treasury bills.
   c. 5-year Treasury notes.
   d. 30-year Treasury bonds.

12. In terms of acceptance by the courts, it is generally agreed that the adjusted-book-value method of valuation is:
   a. Preferred over the market-valuation and discounted-cash-flow methods.
   b. Preferred over the discounted-cash-flow method but not over the market-valuation method.
   c. Less well-accepted than either the market-valuation method or the discounted-cash-flow method.
   d. Equally as well-accepted as the market-valuation and discounted-cash-flow method.

13. Which of the following balance-sheet items are most likely to have adjusted book values that exceed their actual book values: (i) fixed tangible assets; (ii) intangible assets; (iii) accounts receivable; or (iv) raw materials inventory:
   a. i and ii.
   b. ii and iii.
   c. iii and iv.
   d. i and iv.

14. In a minority-interest valuation using the adjusted-book-value method, how should a condominium used exclusively by management be valued if there are no plans for the asset to be sold in the future?
   a. Fair market value.
   b. Book value or discounted fair market value.
   c. A premium above fair market value.
   d. A value of zero.

15. There are many different bases to which discounts and premia are applied. Which of the following describes the value of a firm as a going concern and assumes no changes in the firm's operation, whether or not it is currently operating efficiently?
    a. Third-party sale value.
    b. Freely marketable minority value.
    c. Enterprise value
    d. Gross value.

16. All of the following factors affect the degree of control of majority shareholders *except*:
    a. The financial condition of the firm.
    b. Revenue codes issued by the Internal Revenue Service.
    c. Statutes of the state in which the firm is chartered.
    d. Bond indentures.

17. A good range describing the discount for lack of marketability for the stock of a closely held company (as opposed to a publicly traded firm) is:
    a. 50 to 65 percent.
    b. 35 to 50 percent.
    c. 20 to 35 percent.
    d. 5 to 20 percent.

18. The use of flotation costs as a proxy for the discount for lack of marketability in the case of minority shareholders is:
    a. Appropriate because flotation costs are the only thing standing in the way of marketability.
    b. Inappropriate because minority-interest holders typically are unable to force a public offering
    c. Appropriate because studies have demonstrated a strong correlation between historical marketability discounts and flotation costs on a percentage basis.
    d. Inappropriate because studies have demonstrated a strong inverse relationship between flotation costs and marketability discounts.

19. Fairness opinions typically: (i) provide an opinion about the economic values of an offer to purchase a company; (ii) protect the interests of creditors and employees; (iii) are void of potential conflicts of interest when they are performed by the investment banker of a potential acquired firm; or (iv) are required by law to be conducted prior to an acquisition.
    a. i.
    b. i and ii.
    c. i, ii, and iii.
    d. i, ii, iii, and iv.

20. The value of a minority interest in a private company that pays no dividends has a value closest to:
    a. Enterprise value.
    b. Book value.
    c. Fair value.
    d. Zero.

21. All of the following apply to solvency opinions *except:*
    a. They are important in matters pertaining to leveraged buyouts because of their failure to gain legal credibility in that area.
    b. They protect secured lenders, corporate directors, and selling shareholders from legal action.
    c. They protect unsecured creditors from incurring financial losses.
    d. They require both a valuation and a credit analysis.

22. Which of the following are accepted methods of valuing convertible bonds: (i) find the present value of the expected dividends on the underlying common stock using the required rate of return on the firm's bonds as the discount rate; (ii) combine the value the bond would have if it were straight debt with the value of the option to convert; (iii) multiply the inverse of the required rate of return on the firm's bonds times the EPS of the firm's common stock; or (iv) combine the value of the underlying common stock and the present value of the excess interest received over dividends if the stock were owned.
    a. i and ii.
    b. ii and iii.
    c. iii and iv.
    d. ii and iv.

23. The valuation process for fixed-income securities of closely held companies is very different from the valuation process for common stocks of closely held companies.
    a. True.
    b. False

24. The *Principles of Appraisal Practice* and *Code of Ethics* of the American Appraisal Association specify that, as a minimum, appraisal reports should reveal the name(s) of:
    a. The lead author of the report.
    b. The managing partner or principal of the firm that contracted to perform the appraisal.
    c. All people who provided significant professional assistance in preparing the appraisal.
    d. Both a and b.

25. The *Principles of Appraisal Practice* and *Code of Ethics* of the American Appraisal Association specify that:
    a. Compensation should not be contingent on an action or event resulting from the analysis.
    b. The appraiser should not have an interest in the appraised property.
    c. The appraiser should not be a close relative of the party requesting the appraisal.
    d. All of the above.

26. Which of the following statements is correct concerning key-person discounts and premia:
    a. They apply only if the key person is deceased.
    b. They tend to affect large-company valuations more than small-company valuations.
    c. Key-person premia are non-existent.
    d. They apply only if the key person is living.

Self-Evaluation Answers

1.   c.   See Oliver.

2.   d.   See Oliver.

3.   a.   See Oliver.

4.   a.   See Wolf.

5.   d.   See Wolf.

6.   b.   See Wolf.

7.   c.   See Wolf.

8.   c.   See Gilbert.

9.   d.   See Gilbert.

10.   a.   See Gilbert.

11.   d.   See Gilbert.

12.   c.   See Nicholas.

13.   a.   See Nicholas.

14.   b.   See Nicholas.

15.   c.   See Pratt.

16.   b.   See Pratt.

17.   b.   See Pratt.

18.   b.   See Pratt.

19.   a.   See Gougis.

20.   d.   See Gougis.

21.   a.   See Gougis.

22.   d.   See Budgyk.

23.   b.   See Budgyk.

24.   c.   See Carr.

25.   d.   See Carr.

26.   c.   See Carr.